New Directions for Institutional Research

Paul D. Umbach
EDITOR-IN-CHIEF

J. Fredericks Volkwein
ASSOCIATE EDITOR

Students of Color in STEM

Shaun R. Harper
Christopher B. Newman
EDITORS

Number 148 • Winter 2010
Jossey-Bass
San Francisco

STUDENTS OF COLOR IN STEM
Shaun R. Harper, Christopher B. Newman (eds.)
New Directions for Institutional Research, no. 148
Paul D. Umbach, Editor-in-Chief

Copyright © 2010 Wiley Periodicals, Inc., A Wiley Company

All rights reserved. No part of this publication may be reproduced in any form or by any means, except as permitted under section 107 or 108 of the 1976 United States Copyright Act, without either the prior written permission of the publisher or authorization through the Copyright Clearance Center, 222 Rosewood Drive, Danvers, MA 01923; (978) 750-8400; fax (978) 646-8600. The code and copyright notice appearing at the bottom of the first page of an article in this journal indicate the copyright holder's consent that copies may be made for personal or internal use, or for personal or internal use of specific clients, on the condition that the copier pay for copying beyond that permitted by law. This consent does not extend to other kinds of copying, such as copying for general distribution, for advertising or promotional purposes, for creating collective works, or for resale. Such permission requests and other permission inquiries should be addressed to the Permissions Department, c/o John Wiley & Sons, Inc., 111 River St., Hoboken, NJ 07030; (201) 748-8789, fax (201) 748-6326, http://www.wiley.com/go/permissions.

NEW DIRECTIONS FOR INSTITUTIONAL RESEARCH (ISSN 0271-0579, electronic ISSN 1536-075X) is part of The Jossey-Bass Higher and Adult Education Series and is published quarterly by Wiley Subscription Services, Inc., A Wiley Company, at Jossey-Bass, 989 Market Street, San Francisco, California 94103-1741 (publication number USPS 098-830). Periodicals Postage Paid at San Francisco, California, and at additional mailing offices. POSTMASTER: Send address changes to New Directions for Institutional Research, Jossey-Bass, 989 Market Street, San Francisco, California 94103-1741.

SUBSCRIPTIONS cost $109 for individuals and $280 for institutions, agencies, and libraries in the United States. See order form at end of book.

EDITORIAL CORRESPONDENCE should be sent to Paul D. Umbach, Leadership, Policy and Adult and Higher Education, North Carolina State University, Poe 300, Box 7801, Raleigh, NC 27695-7801.

New Directions for Institutional Research is indexed in *Academic Search* (EBSCO), *Academic Search Elite* (EBSCO), *Academic Search Premier* (EBSCO), *CIJE: Current Index to Journals in Education* (ERIC), *Contents Pages in Education* (T&F), *Current Abstracts* (EBSCO), *EBSCO Professional Development Collection* (EBSCO), *Educational Research Abstracts Online* (T&F), *ERIC Database* (Education Resources Information Center), *Higher Education Abstracts* (Claremont Graduate University), *Multicultural Education Abstracts* (T&F), *Sociology of Education Abstracts* (T&F).

Microfilm copies of issues and chapters are available in 16mm and 35mm, as well as microfiche in 105mm, through University Microfilms, Inc., 300 North Zeeb Road, Ann Arbor, Michigan 48106-1346.

www.josseybass.com

THE ASSOCIATION FOR INSTITUTIONAL RESEARCH was created in 1966 to benefit, assist, and advance research leading to improved understanding, planning, and operation of institutions of higher education. Publication policy is set by its Publications Committee.

PUBLICATIONS COMMITTEE

Gary R. Pike (Chair)	Indiana University–Purdue University Indianapolis
Gloria Crisp	University of Texas at San Antonio
Paul Duby	Northern Michigan University
James Hearn	University of Georgia
Terry T. Ishitani	University of Memphis
Jan W. Lyddon	San Jacinto Community College
John R. Ryan	The Ohio State University

EX-OFFICIO MEMBERS OF THE PUBLICATIONS COMMITTEE

John Muffo (Editor, Assessment in the Disciplines), Ohio Board of Regents
John C. Smart (Editor, Research in Higher Education), University of Memphis
Richard D. Howard (Editor, Resources in Institutional Research), University of Minnesota
Robert K. Toutkoushian (Editor, New Directions for Institutional Research), Indiana University Bloomington
Marne K. Einarson (Editor, AIR Electronic Newsletter), Cornell University
Gerald W. McLaughlin (Editor, AIR Professional File/IR Applications), DePaul University
Richard J. Kroc II (Chair, Forum Publications Committee), University of Arizona
Sharron L. Ronco (Chair, Best Visual Presentation Committee), Florida Atlantic University
Randy Swing (Staff Liaison)

For information about the Association for Institutional Research, write to the following address:

AIR Executive Office
1435 E. Piedmont Drive
Suite 211
Tallahassee, FL 32308-7955

(850) 385-4155

air@mailer.fsu.edu
http://airweb.org

Contents

Issue Editors' Notes 1
  Kathryn Hynes, Barton J. Hirsch

Executive Summary 7

1. Career development during childhood and adolescence 11
  Erik J. Porfeli, Bora Lee
  A review of the literature on how children and adolescents develop career-related identities highlights important considerations for intervention.

2. Teenage employment and career readiness 23
  Kaylin M. Greene, Jeremy Staff
  This article highlights recent research on the prevalence of adolescent employment and its consequences and highlights implications for practice.

3. What schools are doing around career development: Implications for policy and practice 33
  Justin C. Perry, Eric W. Wallace
  This article describes the history of schools' involvement in career programming and identifies promising models for the future.

4. Support for career development in youth: Program models and evaluations 45
  Megan A. Mekinda
  After describing the evaluation findings from four programs offering career development, this article highlights lessons for future program design.

5. Marketable job skills for high school students: What we learned from an evaluation of After School Matters 55
  Kendra P. Alexander, Barton J. Hirsch
  An in-depth exploration of data from the After School Matters evaluation highlights an important component of career programming and a promising area for intervention.

6. Development in youth enterprises 65
  Stephen F. Hamilton, Mary Agnes Hamilton
  This article describes several programs involving youth in enterprises and highlights how these programs connect to important principles of youth development.

7. Building business-community partnerships to support youth development   77
   Donna Klein
   Based on experience working with the private sector, the author suggests ways to build community partnerships, with a special focus on engaging private employers in the effort.

8. Supporting vocationally oriented learning in the high school years: Rationale, tasks, challenges   *85*
   Robert Halpern
   Drawing from diverse research fields, this article highlights the limitations of our current system of education and suggests strategies for improvement.

9. Next steps for research and practice in career programming   *107*
   Kathryn Hynes
   Drawing from the various perspectives presented in this volume, this article highlights areas for further research and practice.

Index   *115*

Issue Editors' Notes

HAVING A WELL-TRAINED workforce is necessary for a healthy economy, productive citizens, and strong families. But there is considerable concern that many of today's youth are not prepared for the demands of the twenty-first-century workforce. Evidence is mounting that we need to think broadly and creatively about how to integrate workforce development and education so that all youth are prepared to participate productively in the labor market of tomorrow.[1]

Indeed, many efforts are under way to improve labor market outcomes for young people. These efforts are being run by secondary schools, out-of-school-time programs, workforce development groups, and postsecondary institutions. Researchers evaluating programs and contributing evidence about how to support career development for youth are publishing in fields as diverse as education, economics, developmental psychology, and sociology. This diversity of perspectives and experiences can be beneficial, but it can also be difficult to identify key research findings and promising program models. This issue of *New Directions for Youth Development* is designed to bring research evidence and promising program models from multiple fields together and encourage discussion about next steps for supporting adolescents' career development.

What is career programming?

Career programming refers to any systematic effort to expose youth to the world of work and teach them the skills and knowledge they need to be successful. It can include career exploration, job search and job readiness skills, supervised work experiences, and technical education. Career programming can be the main focus of a program, or career exploration and skill building can be integrated into a host of content-specific programming in areas such as sports, music, science, and technology. It can be offered during the school day, after school, or in the summer. Career programming should be engaging enough to elicit youth participation and active involvement in the experiences. And ultimately, an effective system of career programming should have long-term impacts on labor market outcomes such as occupational attainment and wages.

Why is career programming important?

Employers report that it is difficult to find the competent, creative workers they need to compete in the global economy. They argue that jobs today require workers who not only can read and write but can evaluate data, solve problems, work on teams, understand complex systems, and apply technology well.[2] In a survey of over four hundred employers, the majority reported that high school graduates were deficient in important workplace skills such as written and oral communication, professionalism, and problem solving.[3]

Postsecondary education is becoming increasingly important for success. Nearly 30 percent of jobs in the future are projected to require some amount of postsecondary education but not a bachelor's degree, and another 33 percent are projected to require a bachelor's degree or higher.[4] But we struggle to keep youth engaged and progressing through the education system. Among youth ages sixteen to twenty-four, an estimated 3.5 to 6 million are high school dropouts.[5] Among high school graduates, some do not enroll in postsecondary education, while others enter postsecondary institutions but do not complete a degree. For instance, only 55 percent of those entering four-year colleges as full-time students completed their degrees within six years, and only 27 percent of those entering two-year institutions completed degrees or certificates in an appropriate time frame.[6] Simply helping youth access the next level of education is not enough to ensure their success.

There is increasing recognition that preparing youth to be productive members of the workforce will require coordinating the efforts of primary and secondary schools, out-of-school-time programs, workforce development programs, employers, and higher education. Strong programming in this area needs to rely on what we know about how youth develop and learn and what engages youth. Given today's economic challenges, it must also cost-effectively improve long-term outcomes.

What does this special issue contribute?

As discussions progress about how to support the career development of youth, we have a considerable research base to draw from. Unfortunately, that research is scattered across a range of disciplines. This issue of *New Directions for Youth Development* brings much of that information together in one place. It presents a mix of broad conceptual and review pieces, new research findings, and examples of promising efforts to engage youth in career-related programming. The articles that follow consider how the institutions around youth can be better designed to support their needs, while keeping the developmental needs and trajectories of young people central.

Issue overview

The first article reviews research on vocational development. Erik J. Porfeli and Bora Lee highlight the importance of career exploration, commitment, and reconsideration across childhood and adolescence, arguing that developmental research should point us toward beginning career programming in childhood and focusing on helping youth establish a vocational identity. The second article highlights the reality that most youth already engage in work through after-school and summer jobs. Kaylin M. Greene and Jeremy Staff review research on the benefits and drawbacks of youth employment and provide guidance for how to promote positive developmental experiences in these early work environments.

The next set of articles focuses on the many ways that institutions are already engaging youth in career-related activities, highlighting what we know about these experiences and how they can best support youth development. Justin C. Perry and Eric W. Wallace review the complex history of public schools' role in career programming, highlighting past efforts, the wide range of ways schools are supporting career development currently, and gaps in our knowledge about what is effective. Megan A. Mekinda reviews a range of programs that have been experimentally evaluated and draws some conclusions about best practices from this research. Kendra P. Alexander and Barton J. Hirsch take a detailed look at the recently evaluated After School Matters program, an apprenticeship program for Chicago high school students. They highlight why particular programs appeared more (and less) successful at improving marketable job skills for youth and describe a new intervention they have been developing.

Engaging youth in career programming at some point needs to involve youth in businesses. Stephen F. Hamilton and Mary Agnes Hamilton define a broad range of youth enterprises, highlight several promising program models, and show how principles for best practices in youth programming can be integrated into youth enterprises. And Donna Klein at Corporate Voices for Working Families draws from the organization's extensive experience to provide schools and community-based organizations with advice about how to collaborate with businesses.

As the other articles show, promising models often involve collaborations across education, workforce development, community-based organizations, and employers. Robert Halpern reviews educational and developmental literature highlighting the importance of vocational learning for youth and identifies key characteristics of quality vocational learning environments, whether they are in schools or in out-of-school settings. He argues that we need to build an integrated system, as youth development happens across settings and over time, and suggests strategies to move from our current system to this more integrated model. The concluding article seeks to integrate many of the ideas raised in this issue, identifying challenging questions and policy implications.

Conclusion

As many of the articles in this issue show, initiatives to promote career readiness are not new: A considerable body of theory, empirical evidence, and practical experience can be drawn from to improve support for youth. This issue provides an interdisciplinary forum to bring together what researchers and practitioners from multiple fields have learned about career programming for youth. The article authors have provided examples of different kinds of career programming and drawn conclusions from the research that can be applied to improve policy and practice. They have also retained a clear developmental focus, placing youth and their needs at the center of the discussion.

We hope this issue will inform the field with up-to-date information from a variety of perspectives and stimulate discussion across disciplines and policy fields about how to best support youth career development.

Kathryn Hynes
Barton J. Hirsch
Issue Editors

Notes

1. Symonds, W., Schwartz, R., & Ferguson, R. (2011). *Pathways to prosperity: meeting the challenge of preparing young Americans for the 21st century.* Cambridge, MA: Harvard Graduate School of Education. Retrieved from http://www.gse.harvard.edu/news_events/features/2011/Pathways_to_Prosperity_Feb2011.pdf

2. U.S. Department of Labor. (1991). *What work requires of schools: A SCANS report for America 2000*. Washington, DC: U.S. Government Printing Office. Retrieved from http://wdr.doleta.gov/SCANS/whatwork/whatwork.pdf

3. Conference Board, Partnership for 21st Century Skills, Corporate Voices, & Society for Human Resource Management. (2006). *Are they ready to work? Employers' perspectives on the basic knowledge and applied skills of new entrants to the 21st century U.S. workforce*. Retrieved from http://www.p21.org/storage/documents/FINAL_REPORT_PDF09-29-06.pdf

4. Carnevale, A., Smith, N., & Strohl, J. (2010). *Help wanted: Projections of jobs and education requirements through 2018*. Washington, DC: Georgetown Center on Education and the Workforce. Retrieved from http://www9.georgetown.edu/grad/gppi/hpi/cew/pdfs/FullReport.pdf

5. Bloom, D., & Haskins, R. (2010). Helping high school dropouts improve their prospects. *Future of Children Policy Brief*. Retrieved from http://futureofchildren.org/futureofchildren/publications/docs/20_01_PolicyBrief.pdf

6. U.S. Department of Education. (2011). *The condition of education: Postsecondary graduation rates*. Retrieved from http://nces.ed.gov/programs/coe/indicator_pgr.asp

KATHRYN HYNES *is an assistant professor of human development and family studies, and demography, at Pennsylvania State University.*

BARTON J. HIRSCH *is a professor of human development and social policy at Northwestern University.*

Executive Summary

Chapter One: Career development during childhood and adolescence
Erik J. Porfeli, Bora Lee

Identity development is central to the career development of children and adolescents. This article reviews the literature pertaining to identity development as being composed of career exploration, commitment, and reconsideration and offers some implications for career interventions.

Chapter Two: Teenage employment and career readiness
Kaylin M. Greene, Jeremy Staff

Most American youth hold a job at some point during adolescence, but should they work? This article presents a broad overview of teenage employment in the United States. It begins by describing which teenagers work and for how long and then focuses attention on the consequences (both good and bad) of paid work in adolescence. It then presents recent nationally representative data from the Monitoring the Future Study suggesting that limited hours of paid work do not crowd out developmentally appropriate after-school activities. A review of the literature also supports the idea that employment for limited hours in good jobs can promote career readiness and positive development. The article concludes with a discussion of the implications of youth work for practitioners and policymakers who are delivering career-related programming.

Chapter Three: What schools are doing around career development: Implications for policy and practice
Justin C. Perry, Eric W. Wallace

This article describes the role that schools are playing in supporting career development for young people. It examines the history of career-related programming in schools, including school-to-work programs, career and technical education, the college and career readiness movement, and current school reform initiatives. This understanding of schools' history, roles, opportunities, and constraints can help practitioners and policymakers think about how to build a system that supports youth development.

Chapter Four: Support for career development in youth: Program models and evaluations
Megan A. Mekinda

This article examines four influential programs—Citizen Schools, After School Matters, career academies, and Job Corps—to demonstrate the diversity of approaches to career programming for youth. It compares the specific program models and draws from the evaluation literature to discuss strengths and weaknesses of each. The article highlights three key lessons derived from the models that have implications for career development initiatives more generally: (1) career programming can and should be designed for youth across a broad age range, (2) career programming does not have to come at the expense of academic training or preparation for college, and (3) program effectiveness depends on intentional design and high-quality implementation.

Chapter Five: Marketable job skills for high school students: What we learned from an evaluation of After School Matters

Kendra P. Alexander, Barton J. Hirsch

This article summarizes findings from an experimental evaluation of After School Matters (ASM), a paid, apprenticeship-based, after-school program in Chicago for high school students. Analysis of quantitative data from a mock job interview revealed that ASM participants did not demonstrate more marketable job skills than youth in the control group. Qualitative data suggested that the nature of interpersonal interactions and the degree of professional orientation in apprenticeships contributed to variation in marketable job skills across apprenticeships. The article considers the perspective of human resource professionals who participated in the evaluation and describes an interviewing skills curriculum developed in response to the evaluation findings.

Chapter Six: Development in youth enterprises

Stephen F. Hamilton, Mary Agnes Hamilton

Business enterprises run by youth can create jobs and teach the principles of free enterprise but also convey skills that can be used by employees in large companies, as well as political activists and entrepreneurs. Research is needed to test the efficacy of this approach and identify its key components.

Chapter Seven: Building business-community partnerships to support youth development

Donna Klein

A confluence of social, economic, and demographic trends has left a generation of young Americans facing an uncertain future in the workforce. If we are to improve their prospects and prepare them for rewarding careers, disparate stakeholders—employers, educators, youth advocates, and others—must work in common purpose. This article suggests ways to build community partnerships, with a special focus on engaging private employers in the effort.

Chapter Eight: Supporting vocationally oriented learning in the high school years: Rationale, tasks, challenges

Robert Halpern

This article highlights the limitations of our current educational system in terms of vocational learning and highlights the role that vocational learning can play in supporting youth development and improving youth outcomes. It discusses the role that nonschool settings can play in supporting vocational learning and suggests strategies to improve our in-school and out-of-school systems to build a more coherent whole that promotes youth development across various settings.

Chapter Nine: Next steps for research and practice in career programming

Kathryn Hynes

The articles in this volume of *New Directions for Youth Development* highlight the broad research base relevant to career programming from which policy and practice can draw. This concluding article integrates these findings to highlight next steps for research and practice related to career programming.

Career development involves establishing and refining a worker identity through exploring, committing to, and reconsidering career alternatives across the life span.

1

Career development during childhood and adolescence

Erik J. Porfeli, Bora Lee

CAREER DEVELOPMENT BEGINS during the childhood period and extends across the life course.[1] It unfolds as an individual establishes a sense of sense of self at work, also known as establishing a vocational identity.[2] Establishing a vocational identity is the response to the question, "Who will I become at work?" The response to this question during childhood is often more gendered and more glamorous than what will follow later.[3] Childhood tasks include learning about the world of work through the work experiences of others, establishing a sense of self, and matching the self with the world of work to establish a budding worker identity. During adolescence, vocational identity development proceeds from a hazy and varnished sense of self relatively detached from a stylized and stereotyped image of work to become a sharper, more realistic, and poignant image of the self at work. The process of refining the self-image is associated with achieving progress on vocational identity development tasks, on the one hand, and improved well-being and diminished distress throughout adolescence and into young adulthood, on the other.[4]

In this article, we offer a general perspective of vocational identity development as central to child and adolescent career development. A review of the pertinent literatures suggests that identity development is the product of three developmental strands—career exploration, commitment, and reconsideration—that appear to begin during childhood and extend into adulthood. We then demonstrate how these three identity processes combine to yield a vocational identity. We conclude with a discussion of the implications of this developmental model of vocational identity development for career interventions.

A process model of vocational identity

Identity development is situated within a developmental model that is presumably preceded by developing a sense of industry and followed by establishing a long-term intimate relationship with a romantic partner.[5] Establishing a strong sense of industry, or the capacity to derive pleasure from work and the worker role, readies children to establish a vocational identity during the adolescent period and predisposes them to exhibit improved well-being during early adulthood.[6] Establishing a strong sense of industry and vocational identity appears to be pivotal because working and working well are central to adult life in modern economies.

Establishing a vocational identity is composed of the tasks of exploring, committing to, and reconsidering career alternatives.[7] These three processes can be used to understand adolescents' and young adults' current identity statuses, which helps identify what should be done to promote vocational identity development.[8] Before proceeding to the discussion about such interventions, we first provide a review of what is known about the exploration, commitment, and reconsideration processes across childhood and adolescence in an effort to establish a rationale for the intervention suggestions that follow.

Career exploration

Identity exploration involves learning broadly and deeply about a particular life domain (for example, friendships, family, religion, work, and politics). Career exploration involves exploring the self and the world of work to obtain a better understanding of the general features of the self and learn about potential career options that might suit these features.[9] Vocational exploration answers the question, "What kinds of work will be suitable to me?" The answer to this question often comes from the work experiences intentionally and unintentionally shared by parents and the media. Youth also try to find an answer to the question by seeking out and learning about careers and the extent to which they might be a more suitable or less suitable choice.[10]

Career exploration presumably proceeds from a broad (in-breadth) exploration of possible vocational identities to increasing deep (in-depth) exploration of core features of the self (interests, values, and life goals, for example) in relationship to specific career opportunities that are perceived as suiting these core features.[11] Young children are exposed to and learn about various careers through textbooks, adults they know, and multimedia sources without having a specific focus on certain careers. Theory suggests that once they find a career that seems interesting to them, they try to learn more about it, seeking out further information from known sources. Both forms of exploration likely operate across the life span as the perceived suitability of career choices and job satisfaction waxes and wanes. Diminished confidence in a career pathway or growing job dissatisfaction may prompt in-breadth exploration (that is, "looking around") that may lead to focused exploration centering on the steps needed to change career goals, prepare for a new career, or make a career transition.

Research supports the distinction between in-breadth and in-depth career exploration but suggests that they have different impacts on career development. In-breadth exploration promotes greater flexibility in approaching a career choice, but it also is associated with a lack of career planning and confidence, especially when the process is prolonged without any experience of in-depth exploration.[12] In-depth exploration has been associated with increasing career planning and confidence, less doubt in one's career choice, and a stronger commitment to a career.[13] Coupled with theories of identity, this research suggests that children and adolescents in the throes of establishing a sense of self may benefit from engaging in a period of in-breadth exploration to the extent that it prevents a premature foreclosure on a career choice that may eventually become less than suitable.[14] On the contrary, adolescents who have established a strong and clear sense of self may benefit from a transition to a period of in-depth exploration as this process tends to lead to a narrowing of alternatives and an eventual commitment to a career.

Career commitment

Career commitment generally has two components: deciding on a career and identifying with it.[15] A career commitment involves making a choice and then attaching one's self to that choice. Career commitment is the product of a process that is presumably rooted in childhood and made manifest at an early age when adults begin to pose the age-old question, "What do you want to do when you grow up?" The response to this question reflects a commitment. Commitment to a career is demonstrated in the decisions (that is, thoughts), choices (that is, behaviors), and vocational identities (that is, a personal connection to one's decisions and choices) that children establish.[16] The answer to this question is often influenced by a number of personal characteristics and most notably by gender, social class, and age.[17] Children tend to identify with jobs that are occupied by people of their gender and social class and tend to be attracted to jobs that are more sensational and glamorous (athlete, model, and movie star, for example) than what they will eventually choose later in life.

Adolescents generally exhibit increasing career decidedness over time, but the pattern is highly variable.[18] The decidedness research suggests that increased decidedness contributes to favorable outcomes like personal adjustment, career maturity, persistence in pursuing an undergraduate degree, and favorable academic and work outcomes.[19] These findings demonstrate that career commitment is an integral part of child and adolescent career development. Combined with theory, these results suggest that career commitment (a career decision coupled with a person connection to the career) is generally a favorable process. However, a premature foreclosure to a career choice before establishing a clear and realistic sense of self can be rather unfavorable in the long term. The ideal timing of a career commitment is contingent on when a person has a clear enough sense of self and sufficient motivation to make it, which suggests that the timing can be different for each individual; in other words, it is difficult to say that there is one perfect period in which to choose a career.

Career reconsideration

Career reconsideration refers to reexamining current commitments and making an effort to compare available alternatives to further specify a career choice or change career choices. Reconsideration can emerge when one has established a career commitment but maintains a flexible attitude toward it. It also occurs when one experiences a self-doubt that often comes from making life-changing decisions.[20] Reconsideration is believed to be a critical process in identity development from the adolescent period onward and is likely to emerge after tentative commitments are made.

Career reconsideration is believed to be reflective of the variability that people tend to exhibit in their career commitments over time.[21] Increased commitment is generally associated with decreased reconsideration, but the process of reconsideration may actually lead to more suitable commitments over the longer term to the extent that it reflects a careful systematic approach to making a career choice.[22] On the positive side, reconsideration can be facilitated by career flexibility, which reflects openness to alternative careers that may emerge over time. On the negative side, reconsideration can be prompted by career self-doubt.[23] Career self-doubt is a tendency to question whether one can achieve a suitable career choice. At the extreme, career self-doubt can breed chronic career indecisiveness and diminished well-being.[24] Indecisiveness has also been shown to limit one from exploring careers.[25] The overall effect of reconsideration of vocational identity is therefore neither good nor bad and hinges on the underlying features of self-doubt and flexibility and the extent to which they dominate one's thoughts, behaviors, and connection to the world of work.

The contemporary world of work is increasingly dynamic and generally favors a more flexible, considerate, self-reflective approach to career commitments.[26] As a consequence, one's vocational identity may become more dynamic over the life course compared to the typical case in the twentieth century.[27] The goal of achieving an increasingly crystallized vocational identity may give way to maintaining a sufficiently adaptable and flexible vocational identity partly as a consequence of ongoing reconsideration through the majority of one's working life. The process of career reconsideration therefore appears poised to become an increasingly important aspect of vocational identity and career development in today's highly changeable world of work.

Exploration, commitment, and reconsideration as three interwoven threads of identity status development

The literature reviewed here suggests that three identity processes may emerge during later childhood, become more pronounced and salient, and mutually influence one another in a complex dynamic fashion across adolescence.[28] The findings suggest that changes in one process may be associated with changes in at least one or both of the other two.

The identity status concept is used to merge the three processes into process patterns and therefore offers a complementary perspective on a person's progress in developing a vocational identity.[29] The six statuses depicted in Figure 1.1 are defined by combinations of career exploration, commitment, and reconsideration. For example, those in the achieved statuses are characterized

Figure 1.1. Vocational identity status model

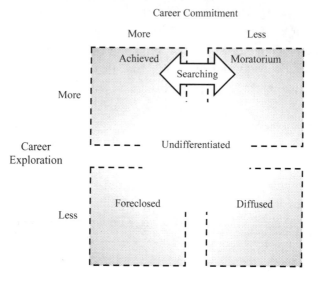

by having explored careers broadly and deeply and being committed to a career. People in this status also report very little reconsideration. The diffused pattern reflects a lack of exploration and commitment with a fair amount of reconsideration. These statuses help to distinguish people in terms of their vocational identity progress; hence, they offer a way of matching people to interventions on the basis of their developmental status. In the next section, we provide examples that show the utility of the statuses and point to a means of assessing adolescents to identify their vocational identity status.

Implications for career interventions

Establishing a vocational identity is a crucial developmental task. That said, the goal for career interventions should be to facilitate vocational identity development, which is basically helping youth understand who they are and finding what careers in the world could fit into their self-images. Several considerations are suggested when developing career interventions that address vocational identity processes or the goal of promoting vocational identity development.

First, the world of work is increasingly dynamic. Learning skills and knowledge about how to establish and revise a vocational identity will prepare youth to adapt to ongoing work and employer changes. While much emphasis is placed on preparing youth for job tasks like problem solving and communication, destabilization of careers in the modern economy dictates that we also prepare our children for lifelong career development tasks like career exploration, commitment, and reconsideration.

Second, vocational identity processes are interwoven, generally moving in a favorable direction over time but highly variable across people. Practitioners should keep in mind that interventions designed to influence any one of the three processes may also have indirect effects on the other two and that they may run into unintended consequences. Interventions designed to strengthen career commitments may also diminish exploration and reconsideration. Interventions to bolster in-breadth career exploration may prompt more reconsideration for those who have already established commitments. We expect increasing commitment and in-depth exploration and decreasing in-breadth exploration and reconsideration over the long term, extending into middle adulthood. The common pattern for children and adolescents will likely reflect a pattern of uneven progress with times of advance and retreat away from establishing a vocational identity, with the long-term trend reflecting progress.

Third, thinking in terms of vocational identity statuses (that is, patterns of identity processes) and shaping interventions to account for the patterns may yield more favorable outcomes. Using an assessment tool, such as the Vocational Identity Status Assessment, to identify identity statuses can be helpful. Vocational identity statuses can be used to direct group-based interventions. Students who went through a lot of exploration and are highly committed to a specific career may benefit from further in-depth career exploration of their career choices coupled with activities that serve to affirm their choices. This group of students may not benefit as much from programs aimed at in-breadth exploration or reconsideration given that this process may erode the gains they have already made in these areas. Adolescents who did not explore enough to make a commitment could benefit from interventions that stimulate thinking broadly about themselves and a range of suitable career choices to facilitate in-breadth career exploration and a focus on general work features that align with their strengths and weaknesses. This group may not benefit from immediate attempts to promote in-depth exploration given that they are less ready to do so, and it may prompt premature foreclosure on a job choice. Youth who have explored but have not settled on a specific career may benefit from activities that prompt progress in terms of commitment. Those who have made a career commitment without any exploration may benefit from some reconsideration of the choice. The point here is that each status lends itself to a slightly different programmatic approach, with the goal being that adolescents generally engage in exploration, commitment, and reconsideration processes before fully establishing a vocational identity.

Fourth, children's contexts should be taken into account. A person-centered intervention, such as personal career counseling and guidance, is likely to be the most effective way to promote vocational identity development partly because the person's environment is likely to be taken into account.[30] However, this can be very costly, so integrating an individualized approach into group-based interventions, much like educators differentiating their instruction to suit various learners, is another way of benefiting from the advantages of one-on-one relationships. If one seeks to intervene with a larger population, there must be some recognition of their contexts and how they support or oppose establishing favorable vocational identities. For example, school counseling programs could create curricula that help students make connections between school subjects and different types of occupations as a way of showing how their learning will apply to the future and how academic strengths and weaknesses align with job imperatives. Community groups such as workforce development organizations and faith-based organizations may contribute by providing career programs that demonstrate job opportunities offered by local businesses. Knowing that job opportunities are available in the community may stimulate adolescents to feel more comfortable in exploring such opportunities in a classroom environment and more confident in making a tentative commitment to one of them. The community context acts as a holding environment for students and their opportunities and constraints. Accounting for them should be considered a focus of intervention efforts directed toward promoting a vocational identity.

Finally, the timing of interventions matters. Traditional career guidance and intervention programs focus on the adolescent years. The lack of career programming for children is often based on the assumption that children are entirely disconnected from the working world. The literature simply fails to support this assumption and in fact shows that preschool children demonstrate an accurate awareness of work.[31] Children develop their interests and values through interaction with family members, teachers, the media, and peers, which in turn has an impact on their broad ideas about work, their career interests, and decisions in later life.[32] Early to late childhood may be the ideal time for career exploration because it is fairly absent of the burden of making an immediate commitment. Moreover, the added time to try out many different options may reduce the uncertainty of commitment, which is usually problematic for older adolescents when the time to make a decision arrives. This last implication may be one of the most important given that many fewer programs exist for children relative to adolescents. This amounts to a missed opportunity for many of our children. In an era when the world of work places increasing pressure on workers to guide their own careers, we may need more time to prepare our children and adolescents for this increasingly important life skill.

Notes

1. Hartung, P. J., Porfeli, E. J., & Vondracek, F. W. (2005). Child vocational development: A review and reconsideration. *Journal of Vocational*

Behavior, 66(3), 385–419; Porfeli, E. J., & Vondracek, F. W. (2009). Career development, work, and occupational success. In M. C. Smith & N. DeFrates-Densch (Eds.), *Handbook of research on adult learning and development* (pp. 412–436). New York, NY: Routledge.

2. Skorikov, V. B., & Vondracek, F. W. (2007). Vocational identity. In V. B. Skorikov & W. Patton (Eds.), *Career development in childhood and adolescence* (pp. 143–168). Rotterdam, Netherlands: Sense Publishers; Savickas, M. L. (2011). Career counseling. In J. Carlson & M. Englar-Carlson (Eds.), *Theories of psychotherapy*. Washington, DC: American Pyschological Association.

3. Goldstein, B., & Oldham, J. (1979). *Children and work: A study of socialization*. New Brunswick, NJ: Transaction Books.

4. Porfeli, E. J., Lee, B., Vondracek, F. W., & Weigold, I. K. (2011). A multi-dimensional measure of vocational identity status. *Journal of Adolescence, 34,* 853–871; Meeus, W. (2011). The study of adolescent identity formation 2000–2010: A review of longitudinal research. *Journal of Research on Adolescence, 21*(1), 75–94.

5. Erikson, E. H. (1968). *Identity: Youth and crisis*. New York, NY: Norton.

6. Skorikov & Vondracek. (2007).

7. Porfeli et al. (2011); Luyckx, K., Goosens, L., Soenens, B., Beyers, W., & Vansteenkiste, M. (2005). Identity statuses based on four rather than two identity dimensions: Extending and refining Marcia's paradigm. *Journal of Youth and Adolescence, 34,* 605–618.

8. Porfeli et al. (2011).

9. Patton, W., & Porfeli, E. J. (2007). Career exploration. In V. B. Skorikov & W. Patton (Eds.), *Career development in childhood and adolescence* (pp. 47–70). Rotterdam, the Netherlands: Sense Publishers.

10. Patton & Porfeli. (2007).

11. Porfeli, E. J. (2008). Career exploration. In F.T.L. Leong (Ed.), *Career counseling* (pp. 1474–1477). Thousand Oaks, CA: Sage.

12. Porfeli et al. (2011); Porfeli, E. J., & Skorikov, V. (2010). Specific and diversive career exploration during late adolescence. *Journal of Career Assessment, 18*(1), 46–58.

13. Porfeli & Skorikov. (2010); Porfeli et al. (2011).

14. Skorikov & Vondracek. (2007).

15. Germeijs, V., Verschueren, K., & Soenens, B. (2006). Indecisiveness and high school students' career decision-making process: Longitudinal associations and the mediational role of anxiety. *Journal of Counseling Psychology, 53,* 397–410.

16. Crites, J. O. (1969). *Vocational psychology: The study of vocational behavior and development*. New York, NY: McGraw-Hill.

17. Hartung et al. (2005).

18. Creed, P. A., Prideaux, L.-A., & Patton, W. (2005). Antecedents and consequences of career decisional states in adolescence. *Journal of Vocational Behavior, 67,* 397–412.

19. Creed et al. (2005); Skorikov, V. B. (2007). Continuity in adolescent career preparation and its effects on adjustment. *Journal of Vocational Behavior,*

70(1), 8–24; Creed, P. A., & Patton, W. (2003). Predicting two components of career maturity in school based adolescents. *Journal of Career Development, 29*, 277–290; Krause, J. A. (1998). *Student-institution fit and its relationship to persistence rates of career decided/undecided first-time freshmen in higher education* (Unpublished doctoral dissertation). University of Wisconsin—Milwaukee; Earl, J. K., & Bright, J.E.H. (2007). The relationship between career decision status and important work outcomes. *Journal of Vocational Behavior, 71*, 233–246.

20. Porfeli et al. (2011).
21. Creed et al. (2005).
22. Porfeli et al. (2011).
23. Porfeli et al. (2011).
24. Gordon, V. N. (1998). Career decidedness types: A literature review. *Career Development Quarterly, 46*, 386–403.
25. Germeijs et al. (2006).
26. Hall, D. T. (2004). The protean career: A quarter-century journey. *Journal of Vocational Behavior, 65*(1), 1–13.
27. Erikson. (1968).
28. Porfeli et al. (2011).
29. Porfeli et al. (2011); Luyckx et al. (2005); Marcia, J. E. (1964). *Determination and construct validity of ego identity status* (Unpublished doctoral dissertation). Ohio State University, Columbus.
30. Savickas. (2011).
31. Hartung et al. (2005).
32. Hartung et al. (2005).

ERIK J. PORFELI *is an associate professor of family and community medicine at Northeast Ohio Medical University.*

BORA LEE *is a doctoral student in human development and family studies at Pennsylvania State University.*

Employment during adolescence can help prepare teenagers for careers in adulthood.

2

Teenage employment and career readiness

Kaylin M. Greene, Jeremy Staff

THE GOAL OF career programming is to ready youth for the world of work. To accomplish this goal, young people are (1) encouraged to consider the type of career they would like to have in adulthood and the schooling needed to pursue it; (2) provided substantive training to develop a particular skill; (3) taught how to find, obtain, and keep a job; and (4) mentored or closely supervised in the workplace. Although youth can learn about the world of work through these career programming initiatives, many adolescents learn about work by holding part-time jobs. Similar to career programming efforts, early workplace experiences can help young people decide what occupations they would like to pursue later in life and what job characteristics are important to them (such as the degree of autonomy, pay, or the chance to help others).[1] Work during adolescence can also provide vocational training and enable young

---

This article uses data from the Monitoring the Future study, which is supported by a grant from the National Institute on Drug Abuse (R01 DA01411). Jeremy Staff is grateful for support from a Mentored Research Scientist Development Award in Population Research from the National Institute of Child Health and Human Development (K01 HD054467). The findings and conclusions in this article are our own and do not necessarily represent the views of the sponsors. Correspondence can be sent to Kaylin Greene, Department of Human Development and Family Studies, The Pennsylvania State University, S110 Henderson Building, University Park, PA 16802–6207.

people to develop soft skills such as punctuality, dependability, and teamwork that employers value.[2] In addition, proponents of youth work have long emphasized that employment can provide opportunities for young people to interact with adult supervisors and coworkers in a structured and productive setting.[3] In short, many teenagers learn about work by working.

In this article, we consider the vocational and developmental benefits of early experiences in paid work, as well as the ways in which working during adolescence may, paradoxically, undermine career readiness. We discuss who works during adolescence and how much and highlight the decline in youth employment during the recent economic recession. We conclude with a discussion on how career programming initiatives can best help teenagers prepare for their future careers.

Entering the workplace

For the majority of youth, work begins early in adolescence.[4] By the eighth grade, for example, many teenagers will have already worked for pay. These first jobs are often informal in character, temporary, and limited in hours; girls typically are employed as babysitters, and boys work in yard maintenance activities. After age sixteen, youth transition into a diverse range of jobs and work intensities (in other words, average weekly work hours). Teenagers typically spend more time working on weekend days and during the summer than on weekdays and during the school year.

Whether and how much teenagers work depends on a number of background factors, such as age, gender, race/ethnicity, and the socioeconomic status of their families.[5] Older teenagers are more likely to work and spend longer hours on the job than younger teenagers. Girls begin work at slightly younger ages than boys, but they average similar hours of work when they do work. Black and Hispanic youth are less likely to work than white youth, but when they do work, they spend longer hours on the job. Youth from disadvantaged family backgrounds are less likely to work than their more advantaged counterparts, but again they average a higher number of hours of work during the week when they are employed.[6]

Early workplace experiences, career readiness, and positive development

Do early workplace experiences help prepare youth for future careers? Is paid work in adolescence developmentally beneficial? There are two sides to this issue. On the one hand is the view that employment at best has little effect on career readiness and social development, and at worst, it leads to poor adjustment and undermines long-term success in the labor market.

In line with the negative view of teenage employment is the popular conception that the jobs available for teenagers are dull and monotonous. When asked to think of a typical teenage job, many Americans conjure up an image of a youth doing repetitive, mindless work in a fast food restaurant. The argument is that teenagers often work in jobs with little career potential, few opportunities for skill development, and no mentorship from adult coworkers or supervisors. In addition, critics have argued that most youth work in age-segregated jobs with their peers. Such jobs may encourage workplace misconduct, foster negative attitudes toward work, and increase the potential for other problem behaviors.[7]

In addition, scholars have argued that youth employment takes time away from other activities that are developmentally beneficial,[8] such as school work, sports participation, and other extracurricular activities.[9] However, research challenges the view that paid work diminishes time spent in other activities, as most teenagers engage in a variety of activities during their out-of-school time. For instance, one common pattern observed during the high school years is that youth combine work with other activities.[10] To illustrate this pattern among contemporary youth, we use data from a nationally representative sample of high school seniors in 2010, from the Monitoring the Future study.[11] Following previous research, we divide the sample into moderate workers (those who work fewer than twenty hours a week during the school year), intensive workers (those who work more than twenty hours), and nonworkers (who average no hours of work). We examine how these groups differ in their leisure and school-related activities.

Youth often engage in a number of activities even when they are working (Table 2.1). Our results suggest that there is not a direct trade-off between time in employment and time in extracurricular activities. Instead, many teenagers engage in daily creative writing, arts and crafts, and music playing regardless of whether they work intensively, moderately, or not at all. In unlisted analyses, we also found that homework time does not vary by employment. Regardless of how much teenagers work, they are equally likely to average an hour or more on homework on a given school day. This suggests that time in other activities does not necessarily suffer because of youth employment. How is this possible? National estimates suggest that youth have approximately eight hours of discretionary time a day, and they devote much of this time to unstructured leisure.[12] Default leisure activities such as TV viewing, which occur when youth have nothing better to do, may be curtailed by youth employment (see Table 2.1). Thus, the large quantity of free time is likely the reason that paid work does not crowd out developmentally beneficial extracurricular activities.

Table 2.1. Percentage of high school seniors engaging in various activities every day by paid work intensity

	Not employed	Moderate workers (1–20 hours per week)	Intensive workers (21 or more hours per week)
Play a musical instrument	35%	35%	31%
Arts and crafts	14	14	14
Read for leisure	28	24	22
Creative writing	10	7	7
Play sports	43	46	38
Watch TV	68	64	58

Source: 2010 Monitoring the Future Survey (Johnston et al., 2011). Authors' calculations.

It is also possible that this pattern of involvement may occur because adolescents save time for activities that they enjoy. If teenagers love a particular activity, they may make an effort to continue engaging in it regardless of whether they are working. Unfortunately, not all extracurricular activities can be easily combined with employment. Consider sports participation. Our findings suggest that intensive workers are less likely to participate in sports than youth who work fewer hours or not at all. This difference may result from the fact that sports participation usually has set practices in which all team members must participate. Moderate workers may be able to successfully balance school sports and employment (by working mostly on the weekends, for instance). However, this may not be an option for intensive workers, as other research has shown.[13] Taken as a whole, our results suggest that youth of varying work intensities often have similar participation in extracurricular activities. When differences do arise, as in the case of sports participation, it is the intensive workers who stand out from the other groups.

Research also demonstrates that many teenage jobs are enjoyable, promote positive development, and have career potential. Many teenage jobs are not dead-end jobs, but instead provide opportunities for skill development, advancement, and interaction and mentorship with adults.[14] In addition to providing youth with important occupation-specific skills, these jobs can also foster the development of soft skills such as dependability, reliability, and punctuality. Good jobs can improve future employment prospects by helping youth develop a network of coworkers who can aid in navigating employment opportunities and serve as references. Consistent with this more positive view, most teenagers and parents hold favorable opinions toward teenage employment. Youth enjoy working, and parents believe that early workplace experiences can provide their children with a number of important skills.[15]

The benefits of teenage employment may be especially important to youth with lower socioeconomic status (SES). Compared to their more advantaged counterparts, youth from disadvantaged backgrounds are more likely to report that their high school job is teaching them useful skills and will lead to a career.[16] Given that youth from low-SES families are also more likely to disengage from school, early work experiences may be an especially salient context for career development for them.[17]

Youth work and the Great Recession

In light of the potential benefits of teenage employment, understanding current employment trends is crucial. Employment trends help to identify which youth are employed and unemployed, enabling practitioners and policymakers to target career-related programming to the most at-risk youth. An analysis of recent trends suggests that the late 2000s were an especially difficult time for youth in the United States. The Great Recession during this time period was particularly severe for certain populations, such as young people. Teenagers often lack education and experience, making them less desirable employees than older workers. Thus, they are often the first to be fired and last to be hired. Indeed, the unemployment rate of teenagers in 2010 was almost three times higher than that of the general population.[18] This high rate paints a somber picture, suggesting that despite a strong desire to work among young people, many still struggled to secure employment. The situation was especially dire for black and Hispanic youth who are severely disadvantaged in the labor market. For instance, in 2010, a whopping 43 percent of black teenagers were unemployed compared to 23 percent of white teenagers.[19]

Analyses from Monitoring the Future further document the dismal employment situation during the late 2000s. For instance, between 2005 and 2010, the number of youth who worked intensively decreased by 9.2 percentage points. In addition, there was a dramatic increase in the percentage of youth reporting no work at all during the school year (from 28.2 percent in 2005 to 41 percent in 2010).[20] These findings suggest that the recession reduced the percentage of youth who were employed as well as the number of hours they worked.

Implications for researchers and practitioners

The discussion has highlighted a number of important points that should be kept in mind when working with or conducting research on adolescents. First, career programming efforts should encourage and help facilitate youth employment, especially in light of the difficulty youth are having finding jobs due to the economic downturn. These efforts should be targeted to youth of lower SES and racial minorities given the high rates of unemployment among these groups. In addition, research suggests that employment does not necessarily crowd out other activities; youth can successfully participate in both types of activities. Although there are some downsides to spending long hours on the job, youth work is likely more beneficial than a drawback.

Although we encourage youth employment, practitioners must nevertheless be cognizant of the many demands on the time of young people. For instance, implementing flexible attendance policies is one solution that might help youth balance multiple obligations to work and school. In addition, given the many activities that take place during the weekdays and during the school year, practitioners might consider how weekend days and summertime could be used as a time for both employment and career-related programming efforts.[21]

Another important consideration relates to the context of work and whether it is good for development. The consequences of teenage work (like other out-of-school contexts) depend on a number of factors related to the quality of the work setting—for example, what kind of work the youth is doing, what skills he or she is learning, and with whom he or she is working. Youth who find and maintain good jobs as teenagers can learn many important skills. Indeed, many of the skills that we hope youth learn during career programming, such as those necessary for the twenty-first-century workforce (teamwork, communication, problem solving) or occupation-specific skills, are often learned through paid work. Policymakers should continue supporting the paid work experiences of disadvantaged youth because they can expose youth to the world of work and the skills they need to succeed in this increasingly complex world.

Finally, career programming efforts should help youth reflect on and learn from their work experiences. What did they like about the job? Would they like to stay in this job in the future? What skills (both job specific and generalizable) did they acquire from it? How did they deal with employment stressors? What techniques did they use to balance work with other life domains such as school and family? Efforts to encourage youth employment and help teenagers learn from these early experiences in the workplace will help them better prepare for future careers.

Notes

1. Mortimer, J. T., Pimentel, E. E., Ryu, S., Nash, K., & Lee, C. (1996). Part-time work and occupational value formation in adolescence. *Social Forces, 74,* 1405–1418.

2. Staff, J., Messersmith, E. E., & Schulenberg, J. E. (2009). Adolescents and the world of work. In R. Lerner & L. Steinberg (Eds.), *Handbook of adolescent psychology* (3rd ed., pp. 270–313). Hoboken, NJ: Wiley.

3. Coleman, J. S., Bremner, R. H., Clark, B. R., Davis, J. B., Eichorn, D. H., Griliches, Z., . . . Mays, J. M. (1974). *Youth: Transition to adulthood.* Chicago, IL: University of Chicago Press.

4. U.S. Department of Labor. (2000). *Report on the youth labor force.* Washington, DC: U.S. Government Printing Office; Staff et al. (2009).

5. National Research Council. (1998). *Youth at work: Health, safety, and development of working children and adolescents in the United States.* Washington, DC: National Academy Press; Porterfield, S. L., & Winkler, A. E. (2007, May). Teen time use and parental education: Evidence from the CPS, MTF, and ATUS. *Monthly Labor Review,* 37–56.

6. U.S. Department of Labor. (2000).

7. Greenberger, E., & Steinberg, L. (1986). *When teenagers work: The psychological and social costs of adolescent employment.* New York: Basic Books.

8. Steinberg, L. D., & Dornbusch, S. M. (1991). Negative correlates of part-time employment during adolescence: Replication and elaboration. *Developmental Psychology, 27,* 304–313.

9. Mahoney, J. L., Vandell, D. L., Simpkins, S. D., & Zarrett, N. (2009). Adolescent out-of-school activities. In R. M. Lerner & L. Steinberg (Eds.),

The handbook of adolescent psychology: Vol. 2. Contextual influences on adolescent development (3rd ed., pp. 228–269). Hoboken, NJ: Wiley.

10. Shanahan, M. J., & Flaherty, B. P (2001). Dynamic patterns of time use in adolescence. *Child Development, 72,* 385–401.

11. Johnston, L. D., Bachman, J. G., O'Malley, P. M., & Schulenberg, J. E. (2011). *Monitoring the Future: A continuing study of American youth (12th-grade survey), 2010.* Ann Arbor, MI: Inter-University Consortium for Political and Social Research.

12. Larson, R. W., & Verma, S. (1999). How children and adolescents spend time across the world: Work, play, and developmental opportunities. *Psychological Bulletin, 125,* 701–736; Wight, V. R., Price, J., Bianchi, S. M., & Hunt, B. R. (2009). The time use of teenagers. *Social Science Research, 38,* 792–809.

13. Safron, D. J., Schulenberg, J. E., & Bachman, J. G. (2001). Part-time work and hurried adolescence: The links among work intensity, social activities, health behaviors, and substance use. *Journal of Health and Social Behavior, 42,* 425–449.

14. Mortimer, J. T. (2003). *Working and growing up in America.* Cambridge, MA: Harvard University Press.

15. Phillips S., & Sandstrom K. L. (1990). Parental attitudes toward youth work. *Youth and Society, 22,* 160–183.

16. Mortimer. (2003).

17. Entwisle, D. R., Alexander, K. L., & Olson, L. S. (2000). Early work histories of urban youth. *American Sociological Review, 65,* 279–297.

18. U.S. Bureau of Labor Statistics. (2011). *Labor force characteristics by race and ethnicity, 2010* (Report 1032). Retrieved from www.bls.gov/cps/cpsrace2010.pdf

19. U.S. Bureau of Labor Statistics. (2011).

20. Bachman, J. G., Johnston, L. D., & O'Malley, P. M. (2011). *Monitoring the Future: Questionnaire responses from the nation's high school seniors, 2010.* Ann Arbor, MI: Institute for Social Research.

21. Hynes, K., Constance, N., Greene, K., Lee, B., & Halabi, S. (2011). *Engaging youth in career programming during out-of-school time.* Retrieved from http://www.psaydn.org/Documents/PSAYDNCareerProgramming.pdf

KAYLIN M. GREENE *is a graduate student pursuing a dual Ph.D. in human development and family studies and in demography at the Pennsylvania State University.*

JEREMY STAFF *is an associate professor of crime, law, and justice, and sociology at the Pennsylvania State University.*

Against the policy backdrop of the college and career readiness movement and historical tensions between the role of education and the needs of the workforce, schools are natural settings to provide a variety of career programming for youth, especially students who are at greatest risk for school dropout.

3

What schools are doing around career development: Implications for policy and practice

Justin C. Perry, Eric W. Wallace

SCHOOLS CAN SERVE as a centralized hub for the coordination and delivery of career programming.[1] As one approach to reform in education, it is an effective, albeit overlooked, solution to underachievement and school dropout rates.[2] While this article focuses on the role of schools, school-based career programs are most comprehensively understood as one of multiple services that can, and often should, be provided in tandem with other academic and nonacademic programs provided across multiple settings.

Correspondence regarding this article can be directed to Justin C. Perry, Associate Professor, CASAL Department, Director, Center for Urban Education, by telephone at 216–687–5424, or by e-mail at j.c.perry96@csuohio.edu

The silent epidemic: A call for college and career readiness

Policy analysts have referred to high school dropout rates as a "silent epidemic."[3] In particular, the "dropout factories" of America have reached crisis proportions in the urban schools, which have disproportionate concentrations of low-income, racial, and ethnic minority youth.[4] In response to this national crisis, the Obama administration pledged to reverse the course of school dropout rates, calling it an "economic imperative" if America is to be competitive in the new global knowledge-based economy.[5] Because nearly three-fourths of dropouts are youth of color and because only 10 percent of them who enroll in college graduate, it is critical to focus reform efforts on this high-need population.[6]

In 2010, over 1 million students did not graduate from high school.[7] The lost lifetime earnings in wages, taxes, and work productivity for that class of dropouts alone totals approximately $337 billion.[8] Although progress in improving the graduation rates of schools with less than 60 percent promoting power has been made over the past ten years, the rate of improvement is still too slow. To accelerate the pace, stakeholders have been directing their attention to a wide range of initiatives. The Grad Nation campaign, launched in 2010, led to the creation of what has been referred to as a "civic Marshall Plan" designed to end the school dropout epidemic. Among its action plans and components, college and career readiness figures prominently. Moreover, the Common Core State Standards now being adopted by nearly every state in the country is explicitly devoted to preparing students for college and careers. The term *college and career readiness* is so widespread that it has become the underlying mantra of any education reformer or advocate on the left or the right of the political spectrum. Indeed, this term often goes hand-in-hand with another popular buzzword: *twenty-first-century skills*.

The concept of twenty-first-century skills is embodied within the learning framework espoused by the Partnership for 21st Century Skills (P21), a national organization that advocates for twenty-first-century readiness. Underpinning its holistic view of teaching and learning, P21 proposes a blending of academic subjects with twenty-first-century themes, including learning and innovation skills, information, media and technology skills, and life and career skills.

Amid this climate of urgency, school-based career programs have the capacity to address the most pressing problems we face in education with a compelling rationale and a solid foundation of empirical evidence. Although this programming is by no means the answer to all problems in K-12 education, it can be a cost-effective and sustainable solution with a high impact in the effort to end the silent epidemic through a targeted, multipronged approach. Today the themes that dominate the academic and policy debates are partially a recycling of ideas from the past. The academic language and dialogue have shifted over time, but the fundamental tensions between learning academic skills and applying what is learned in school to the workforce have remained constant.

Education and work: A historical relationship

During the early and mid-1800s, instruction in core areas of language, math, science, and history stood as the basic type of formal education, primarily reserved for the affluent. The reality was that most children attended school for only a few years, and a very small percentage of Americans went to college. At the turn of the twentieth century, the classical approach to school was overtaken by a hands-on philosophy of preparing a massive number of students for employment in industry after their graduation.[9] As the need grew for line workers who could perform laborious tasks in an efficient, regimented manner, it gave rise to the concept of vocational education. Public schools of the early 1900s, funded by the Smith-Hughes Act of 1917, bore the responsibility for preparing compliant and reliable workers to meet the demands of factories, mills, offices, and stores.

The birth of occupational and technical training did not eradicate exam schools. Rather, it basically divided academic training into a vocational track and a college preparation track. Vocational education came to be criticized, unfairly or not, as a second-rate alternative to schooling, allegedly reinforcing class boundaries.[10] This bifurcation of tracks set the stage for modern debate in education around rigor versus relevance, or academic standards versus real-world applications. To rectify the dualistic system, career education emerged during the 1970s as an approach for programs aimed at enhancing the occupational relevance of education. In the 1970s, wages declined across all sectors of the labor force. Driving this decline was the increasing use of automation and computer technology, thus reducing the need for semiskilled and unskilled workers.[11] The information age profoundly changed the nature of almost every service industry. The new world order turned into globalization and open markets.

In 1990, the National Center on Education and the Economy published *America's Choice: High Skills or Low Wages!* The report pointed to a crossroad our nation had reached that was due to the dissolving need for unskilled labor and a widened achievement gap based on race and income. Specifically, the conclusion was that America had to choose between offering all young people the opportunity to develop high skills or consign the majority of students to a bleak path of low wages and little chance for promotion.

After *A Nation at Risk* was published in 1983, reforms focused on preparing students for higher education.[12] Throughout the 1980s, dozens of reports enjoined states to upgrade the academic proficiencies of college-bound students in language, math, and science, while virtually ignoring the needs of work-bound youth.[13] In 1988, the William T. Grant Foundation Commission on Work, Family, and Citizenship issued its report known as *The Forgotten Half*. In contrast to *A Nation at Risk*, the data showed that over half of U.S. high school graduates did not attend college. *The Forgotten Half*, published in 1988, marked a turning point in educational reform, which materialized into a consensus that schools must prepare all students for success in life.[14] The report inevitably brought policymakers and social scientists to the realization that schools were failing to prepare a large segment of the population for high-skill, high-wage jobs. After the 1990 Amendments to the Perkins Vocational Education Act of 1984, the National Assessment of Vocational Education and the Secretary's Commission on Achieving Necessary Skills (SCANS) in 1991 ushered in a new era of career education.

During the same period of *The Forgotten Half* and the rise of the SCANS report, the precursor to what has become known as twenty-first-century skills, the school-to-work (STW) movement was also conceived. Originally it focused on students who do not immediately embark on a four-year college degree, and then expanded to include students going to college as well. The School-to-Work Opportunities Act (STWOA) of 1994, which incorporated the work-based competencies outlined in the SCANS report, was passed with bipartisan support in response to the rapidly changing needs of the workplace; it provided seed money for states and local communities to create partnerships with businesses, community colleges, universities, and technical schools. The STWOA delineated three components for any STW system: school-based learning, work-based learning, and connecting activities designed to strengthen linkages between school and work. Although STWOA expired in 2001, its basic philosophical underpinnings inform current approaches to career programming.[15] The Carl D. Perkins Career and Technical Education Act, reauthorized in 2006, attests to the integration of school and the workforce, providing states with funds to support career and technical education, operating expenses, innovation, and program improvement.

Common models of career programs in schools

The overarching scheme of integrating school and work has taken on various manifestations over the past several decades. The following models are common ones that are used nationwide:[16]

- *Career academies.* Schools function as either small schools within a comprehensive school or as separate schools, typically serving between 150 and 200 students and starting at the ninth or tenth grade. The curriculum is organized around a broad career theme (for example, health science, arts, or business); the same cohort of students and group of teachers stay together for several years. Students may participate in work-based learning. Established in 1970, career academies may be viewed as being interchangeable with similar models known as career magnets, career majors, or small learning communities. These terms refer to a model of education in which students take a sequence of courses organized around a career area.
- *Technical preparation programs.* Students combine the last two years of high school with two years in a community college and earn a technical degree. They may or may not participate in work-based learning.
- *Early college high schools.* This model consists of small schools located primarily on college campuses. The basic goal is to provide a high school diploma and an associate degree, or two years of transferable college credit.
- *School-based enterprises.* Students identify and address community needs in the form of service-learning projects.

Based on findings from the Pathways to Prosperity Project, young people are not benefiting from the traditional model that emphasizes going to a four-year college as the best or only route to success ("college for all"). Instead, the authors champion the case for offering multiple pathways to success as a better approach to school reform. Despite the college-for-all mandate, only 40 percent of twenty-seven year olds earn an associate degree or higher; most jobs do not even require a four-year degree.[17] According to the Center on Education and the Workforce at Georgetown University, about 67 percent of jobs projected in 2018 will not require a bachelor's or a graduate degree.[18] Although the "ticket to success" surely requires education and training beyond high school, a four-year degree does not guarantee a high-earning job or employment. Indeed, other paths to prosperity may be more realistic and rewarding in ways that more effectively suit youths' interests, goals, and skills.

The contemporary models listed above represent the multiple pathways approach to the STW transition, which has evolved into the "college and career readiness" movement. In essence, college and career readiness encompasses the basic ideas of STW articulated over fifteen years ago. There are many examples of promising school-based models that embrace the tenets of career education, but on a nationally comprehensive scale, such examples are few and far between. Eventually, sweeping reforms will have to take hold over the fragmented approach to career programming we see today.

Career programming in action: Ohio and beyond

In this section, we illustrate current trends within schools in the state of Ohio. In doing so, we comment on the implications for these models, including the opportunities and challenges for public policy, implementation, accountability, and bringing practice to scale.

Like other states, Ohio receives funding from Perkins IV, or the Carl D. Perkins Career and Technical Education Act of 2006, which focuses on the academic achievement of career and technical students while improving state and local accountability. Currently the state disburses these funds to facilitate the pursuit of three forms of career and technical education (CTE): tech prep, High Schools That Work (HSTW), and career based-intervention (CBI) for at-risk youth. Ohio is the twenty-second state to adopt the HSTW national initiative to improve student success through vocational education.

At Penta Career Center in Perrysburg, Ohio, for example, twenty-eight career-training programs are offered to high school juniors and seniors in six core areas; some programs also offer dual-enrollment options to earn college credit. Students earn academic credit for half the day, and the second half is devoted to vocational training. Similar to the HSTW initiative and career based programming, however, tech prep schools like the Penta Career Center often lack research-based evidence to support their effectiveness in improving achievement and postsecondary or labor market outcomes. The noticeable gap in providing rigorous program evaluation reflects criticisms of CTE programs (and the Perkins Act) in general. Establishing a uniform base of quality assurance metrics and outcomes tracked longitudinally would enable stakeholders to not only show that these programs work, but also allow them to understand why and how they work, including ways in which they can be improved and replicated. Currently the CTE state targets and performance for Perkins IV indicators at the secondary and post-secondary level are based on counts of "output" rather than "outcome." For example, academic attainment is assessed by counting the number of CTE students scoring at or above proficiency on the Ohio Graduation Test (OGT), divided by the number of CTE students who took the test. The fraction of students who scored at or above proficiency, however, cannot tell us how effective the programs actually were in causing CTE students in Ohio to do better on these tests compared to a similar population of non-CTE students.

One of the Cleveland Metropolitan School District's new innovation schools, MC²STEM High School, is a project-based school located on an industry corporate campus at GE Lighting's Nela Park. Its freshman campus is located at the Great Lakes Science Center. Students have opportunities to job-shadow and intern in fields related to science, technology, engineering, and mathematics (STEM); they can also take college courses. MC²STEM provides a year-round academic calendar so as to reinforce what students can expect from work life. Compared to the district's students who scored at or above the proficiency level on the OGT in 2010–2011 for mathematics in the tenth (58.7 percent) and eleventh grades (73.6 percent), MC²STEM students performed at 85 percent and 93.8 percent, respectively. For the Science OGT, MC²STEM's tenth- and eleventh-grade results (81.7 and 86.2

percent) were higher than those of the district (44.3 and 62.1 percent).

Although these facts are impressive, there is no evidence to conclude how the impact on the OGT can be attributed to MC²STEM as opposed to the unique characteristics of its students. Aside from the need for evaluation designs with comparison or control groups, schools like MC²STEM must eventually demonstrate cost-effectiveness. Bringing these dynamic models to scale must take into account how its core elements can be maintained, while other features can be curtailed or implemented in flexible and efficient ways. Not every school will be in a position to enjoy the same access to facilities and similar contributions from the private sector and philanthropic institutions. A right-sized or appropriately distilled version, so to speak, may be required for other districts and schools that wish to adopt the model but with fewer resources available to implement it.

Of course, breaking traditional large, comprehensive high schools into autonomous career academies and variations of CTE may not always be possible within a district or suitable for a particular population. Furthermore, middle school students and high school freshmen are often enrolled in large schools before entering such academies if they are available. The model of ninth-grade academies underscores the widely recognized importance of the eighth-to-ninth-grade transition, as well as the transition from ninth grade to a smaller learning community as critical periods in which youth are most vulnerable to dropping out or disengaging from school. In response to these equally pressing needs, the first author has collaborated with English language arts teachers from five urban high schools to design, implement, and evaluate an innovative school dropout prevention program that targets disadvantaged youth, especially freshmen entering high school: Making My Future Work (MMFW). The program will serve over four hundred students across two years in its pilot testing phase.

A distinctive feature of MMFW is that it can be used within the general English language arts curriculum as a universal intervention that is delivered during regular school hours of operation.

Thus, it is applicable for students with interests in any career or occupation, regardless of the school academic structure (e.g., career academy, tech prep, general curriculum) in which it is implemented. Because students will still need to learn how to read and write and meet basic requirements in literature before graduating, MMFW is accessible for all types of students across a wide range of academic programs in the secondary education system. So far, MMFW contains over fifty lesson plans under three themes: self-exploration, career exploration, and twenty-first-century skills. It also has joined with nonprofit agencies that provide employment services and summer jobs to low-income youth, as well as college access advising. MMFW synthesizes the contributions of the SCANS report and the STWOA Act in its developmental, comprehensive approach to college and career readiness programming for youth of all grade levels in secondary education.

Teachers have the flexibility and autonomy to choose which lessons from the manual they want to implement as long as the lessons target specific goals for a minimum number of times over a minimum duration of time. Each lesson is directly aligned with the new Common Core State Standards and is seamlessly integrated within the English language arts curriculum. These interdisciplinary and interprofessional efforts have mitigated the risk of not being able to gain buy-in from administrators and teachers, a common obstacle when trying to introduce a program into the existing bureaucracy and traditions of a school system. Yet the road to future replication still presents challenges: MMFW, like any other innovative comprehensive program, must be broad-based enough to convince other superintendents, principals, and teachers with different needs and circumstances in their schools. The convincing can in part be solved through research-based evaluation results but must also be sold, so to speak, with easy-to-navigate products, materials, and hands-on training resources. These challenges require that like-minded educators and helping professionals be open to many perspectives from multiple stakeholders, even those that are not congruent with their own views or professional background. They must collaborate with partners in other specialties who offer skills and insight in areas such as classroom instruction, learning theory, educational technology, marketing, multimedia, teacher professional development, and curriculum design.

Conclusion

Given the magnitude of the silent epidemic and the complex challenges young people face in the global economy, it would be misleading to suggest that career programming in the schools can function as a panacea. Rather than viewing this approach as a grand vaccine that will protect youth from a lifetime of adversity, we should treat it as one of many consecutive, coordinated, and targeted flu shots, if you will, that can serve as an antidote with the necessary resources and investments from K-12 education, higher education, the private sector, nonprofits, and youth agencies.

Notes

1. Walsh, M. E., & Galassi, J. P. (2002). An introduction: Counseling psychologists and schools. *Counseling Psychologist, 30,* 675–681.
2. Baker, S. B., & Taylor, J. G. (1998). Effects of career education interventions: A meta-analysis. *Career Development Quarterly, 46,* 376–385; Evans, J. H., & Burck, H. D. (1992). The effects of career education interventions on academic achievement: A meta-analysis. *Journal of Counseling and Development, 71,* 63–68; Wilson, S. J. (2011). *Effects of prevention and intervention programs on school completion and dropout: Results from a systematic review.* Paper presented at the Society for Research on Educational Effectiveness Conference, Washington, DC.
3. Bridgeland, J. M., DiIulio, J. J., & Morison, K. B. (2006). *The silent epidemic: Perspectives of high school dropouts.* Washington, DC: Civic Enterprises.
4. Balfanz, R., & Legters, N. (2004). *Locating the dropout crisis: Which high schools produce the nation's dropouts? Where are they located? Who attends them?* Baltimore, MD: Johns Hopkins University.
5. Zeleny, J. (2010, March 1). Obama takes aim at school dropout rates. *New York Times.* Retrieved from http://thecaucus.blogs.nytimes.com/2010/03/01/obama-takes-aim-at-school-dropout-rates/
6. America's Promise Alliance. (2011). *Dropout prevention.* Retrieved from http://www.americaspromise.org/Our-Work/Dropout-Prevention.aspx
7. Alliance for Excellent Education. (n.d.). *Education and the economy: Boosting local, state, and national economies by improving high school graduation rates.* Retrieved from http://www.all4ed.org/publication_material/Econ

8. Balfanz, R., Bridgeland, J. M., Moore, L. A., & Foz, J. H. (2010). *Building a grad nation: Progress and challenge in ending the high school dropout epidemic.* Baltimore, MD: Civic Enterprises, Johns Hopkins University, and America's Promise Alliance.

9. Marshall, R., & Tucker, M. (1992). *Thinking for a living: Education and the wealth of nations.* New York: Basic Books.

10. Blustein, D. L., Perry, J. C., & DeWine, D. (2004). School-to-work transition. In C. Spielberger (Ed.), *Encyclopedia of applied psychology* (Vol. 3, pp. 351–353). Orlando, FL: Academic Press.

11. Schweke, W. (2004). *Smart money: Education and economic development.* Washington, DC: Economic Policy Institute.

12. National Commission on Excellence in Education. (1983). *A nation at risk: The imperative for educational reform.* Washington, DC: U.S. Department of Education.

13. Smith, C. L., & Rojewski, J. W. (1993). School-to-work transition: Alternatives for educational reform. *Youth and Society, 25,* 222–250.

14. The Forgotten Half: Pathways to Success for America's Youth and Young Families. (1988, November). Final report of the William T. Grant Foundation Commission on Work, Family, and Citizenship. Washington, DC.

15. Blustein, D. L., Juntunen, C. L., & Worthington, R. L. (2000). The school-to-work transition: Adjustment challenges of the forgotten half. In S. D. Brown & R. W. Lent (Eds.), *Handbook of counseling psychology* (3rd ed., pp. 435–470). Hoboken, NJ: Wiley.

16. It should be noted that work-based learning models, including cooperative education, job shadowing, internships and apprenticeships, and work-based mentoring, may or may not be tied to career programs delivered in the schools. Ideally, school- and work-based learning are systematically connected throughout the curriculum.

17. Symonds, W. C., Schwartz, R. B., & Ferguson, R. (2011, February). *Pathways to prosperity: Meeting the challenge of preparing young Americans for the 21st century.* Cambridge, MA: Harvard Graduate School of Education.

18. Carnevale, A. P., Smith, N., & Strohl, J. (2010, June). *Help wanted: Projections of jobs and education requirements through 2018.* Washington, DC: Center on Education and the Workforce, Georgetown University.

JUSTIN C. PERRY *is the director of the Center for Urban Education and an associate professor in the Department of Counseling, Administration, Supervision, and Adult Learning at Cleveland State University.*

ERIC W. WALLACE *is a doctoral student in the counseling psychology program at Cleveland State University.*

This overview of four program models demonstrates the diversity within career programming and highlights important considerations for the continuing development and implementation of initiatives for youth.

4

Support for career development in youth: Program models and evaluations

Megan A. Mekinda

CAREER PROGRAMMING TAKES many forms. It can include any combination of career exploration, skill development, and counseling. It can take place in schools, workplaces, or community centers. It can be intensive and the explicit focus of an initiative or casual and a single component of a more comprehensive program. And it can target individuals of any age, ability, or aspiration. In this article, I present four examples of career programming for youth. The programs—Citizen Schools, After School Matters, career academies, and Job Corps—were selected to demonstrate the diversity among approaches. However, all are exemplary in that they employ a number of theory-driven and evidence-based practices, many of which inform broader education reform initiatives. These include opportunities for project-based or experiential learning; the integration of academic, social, and technical skills; the creation of networks of supportive adults and peers; and partnerships among institutions, easing the burden on schools to prepare youth for an increasingly competitive and ever-changing job market. Importantly, the programs predominantly serve low-income and minority youth, mainly from urban areas, who often have quite limited access to supports for career development.

The effectiveness of these programs has implications for the continued development and implementation of career programming initiatives for youth. Therefore, I draw from evaluation research to examine the programs' impact on outcomes related to career development. Each program has been the subject of a large-scale external evaluation. Three (After School Matters, Career Academies, and Job Corps) have undergone an experimental trial in which researchers randomly assigned interested youth to the program (treatment) or business as usual (control) and assessed differences in their outcomes. This design is the gold standard in evaluation research because it effectively eliminates the possibility that the observed effects reflect preexisting differences between program participants and nonparticipants rather than the impact of the program itself. Despite their benefits, experimental trials are notoriously difficult to implement and consequently quite rare. Therefore, the programs presented in this chapter are unusual in terms of the rigor of their evaluations. I conclude the chapter with three key lessons derived from these models that have implications for career development initiatives more generally.

Citizen Schools

Citizen Schools is an expanded learning time initiative for low-income youth in grades 6 through 8. Founded in Boston in 1995, the program has since expanded to eighteen cities across seven states and serves approximately forty-five hundred youth every year. Participants meet ten weeks a semester, four days a week, three hours a day.

With its focus on middle schoolers, Citizen Schools is clearly not designed to prepare youth for immediate entry to the workforce. Rather, the program is weighted heavily toward support for academic achievement, with the goal of enrolling students into top-tier high schools along the pathway to college and eventually careers. Accordingly, each session includes structured homework and study time supervised by program staff. Explicit attention to career development comes in the form of apprenticeships offered one day a week. Apprenticeship instructors are volunteers from the community—professionals, businesspeople, and others—who lead students in hands-on activities related to their area of expertise, from fine arts and architecture to finance, science, and technology. Youth are exposed to possible career fields and adult mentors while practicing problem solving, collaboration, and other key skills. Apprenticeships culminate in a public performance or demonstration in which students showcase their work. A series of college-to-career connection activities (for example, campus visits) are designed to help youth grasp the relationship of their academic performance, college, and careers so they can make informed choices at all points along the pathway.

Policy Studies Associates recently completed a longitudinal evaluation of Citizen Schools in Boston, tracking alumni of the 8th Grade Academy, the capstone program to support students' transition to high school.[1] The study was quasi-experimental: instead of randomly assigning youth to treatment, the researchers compared Citizen Schools participants to nonparticipants matched according to selected characteristics such as gender and academic ability. Thus, findings should be regarded cautiously since they might reflect unobserved differences between participants and nonparticipants (for example, regarding motivation). However, the consistency and strength of the results are promising in terms of the program's support for school engagement, academic performance, and progress toward graduation. Citizen Schools alumni were significantly more likely to enroll and persist in top-tier high schools, they had higher high school attendance rates, and they demonstrated gains in math and English language arts performance. Alumni were also significantly more likely than program nonparticipants to graduate from high school on time. Although the evaluation did not include any measures specific to career development, such as career plans or nonacademic skills, findings suggest that the Citizen Schools model helps students attain key educational milestones along the pathway to college and careers.

After School Matters

After School Matters (ASM) in Chicago is widely considered the flagship program for high school youth and is perhaps the largest single-city after-school program for this age group in the country. Founded in 2000, ASM serves the city's public school students, the vast majority of whom are low income and minority. It currently offers more than fifty-five hundred apprenticeship opportunities each semester in forty-five high schools.

Like Citizen Schools, ASM engages youth in apprenticeships led by professionals from the community with expertise in a broad range of occupations and career fields. Unlike Citizen Schools, programming hours are dedicated entirely to apprenticeship activities, with virtually no explicit focus on academic achievement. The program prioritizes the development of marketable job skills, both hard skills specific to a trade as well as soft skills (like teamwork) that generalize across work environments. The ASM model is meant to simulate characteristics of the professional workplace, for example, through the creation of a product or performance to be consumed by others, the imposition of deadlines, and the award of a stipend for participation. However, most programs are based in schools, which means students have limited access to actual work environments. Furthermore, many apprenticeships focus on the fine and performing arts, occupations not well aligned with industry demands, as is more the case with career academies and Job Corps. However, the intensity and duration of ASM (three hours a day, three days a week, ten weeks a semester) create opportunities for youth to form meaningful, and ideally, mentor-like relationships with adults who can provide advice and guidance for careers and life. Students' prolonged engagement in project-based and experiential learning also creates opportunities for skill development.

To date, the most rigorous assessment of After School Matters is the experimental evaluation by Hirsch and colleagues.[2] Using a sample of thirteen of the program's strongest apprenticeships, the study examined differences between treatment and control youth on measures of marketable job skills and positive youth development, ASM's priority outcomes, as well as indicators of academic achievement and problem behavior. (See Alexander and Hirsch, this issue, for details of the mock job interview, the evaluation's measure of marketable job skills, and related findings.) Findings revealed significant and favorable program effects for only two outcomes: self-regulation, a component of positive youth development that reflects one's ability to manage attention and emotion, and problem behavior, particularly gang activity and selling drugs. The authors interpret the findings as modest but promising, particularly since nearly all control youth were involved in alternative after-school activities, raising the bar for ASM. Furthermore, the program is fairly young and committed to the continued improvement of its model. The null findings with regard to marketable job skills and academic achievement suggest that more progress is necessary to support these key components of career development.

Career academies

Whereas Citizen Schools and ASM capitalize on out-of-school time, career academies represent an in-school initiative to prepare youth for college and careers. Participants enroll from two to four years during high school, earning credit toward graduation. The first academy opened in Philadelphia in 1969, and today more than twenty-five hundred exist nationwide. Although there is some variation among individual academies, the recognized model has three features: (1) a school-within-a-school organization, or small learning community; (2) the integration of occupational and academic curricula, usually college preparatory; and (3) partnerships with local employers who provide a range of support, including curriculum advising, sponsorship of work-based learning opportunities such as job shadowing and internships, and student mentoring.

Today's career academies should be distinguished from more traditional approaches to vocational education. Academies target students from a broad range of academic abilities, not just those at risk of dropping out of high school, and engage them in both vocational and academic training. Fields include technology, finance, and health care, which have a high demand for skilled workers and often require some form of postsecondary education. Indeed, many students have college aspirations, and academies can help to facilitate this by providing opportunities to earn scholarship money or developing articulated curricula with local colleges.

The largest and most rigorous evaluation of career academies was completed by Kemple and colleagues from MDRC.[3] They employed an experimental design to study the effects of nine academies across the nation, tracking outcomes for eight years after the youth's scheduled high school graduation. Findings indicate positive effects of career academies on participants' experiences during high school, including greater interpersonal support and participation in career awareness and work-based learning activities. Although impacts on academic achievement were weak for the sample as a whole, youth at high risk of school failure experienced significant gains: they had lower high school dropout rates and higher attendance and were more likely to be on track to graduate. Academies did not have a significant impact on students' standardized test scores, high school graduation rates, enrollment in postsecondary education, or employment immediately after high school. However, there were long-term impacts: academy participants experienced significant earnings gains eight years after their scheduled high school graduation. Benefits were particularly strong for young men, who reported higher wages, more hours worked, and greater employment stability, resulting in an earnings gain of 17 percent. The researchers conclude that career academies, when fully implemented, contribute positively to labor force preparation and school-to-work transitions.

Job Corps

Founded in 1964, Job Corps is a program administered by the U.S. Department of Labor (DOL) to promote economic self-sufficiency, employability, and responsibility among youth. To qualify, participants must be low income, between the ages of sixteen and twenty-four, and a legal U.S. resident. Job Corps serves sixty thousand new participants each year across forty-eight states, the District of Columbia, and Puerto Rico, making it the largest education and vocational training program for disadvantaged youth in the country.

Of the programs considered in this article, Job Corps is also the most intensive and comprehensive. It offers classroom-based academic training for credit toward a high school diploma or General Educational Development (GED) credential; hands-on and work-based vocational training for credit toward vocational certifications; and a range of additional services, including meals, basic health care, counseling, and recreation. Services are concentrated in Job Corps centers (there are 125 nationwide) in areas where the majority of participants also live. The program is individualized and self-paced, so participants can take advantage of services according to their need. The duration of enrollment varies by individual and averages eight months.

In addition to enrolling young adults, Job Corps is the only program of the four examined here that caters specifically to youth who are disengaged from school, the majority of whom are high school dropouts. Consequently, it is more focused on preparing participants for immediate entry to the workforce. The program provides job placement services for up to six months after youth exit the program.

In the mid-1990s, the DOL sponsored a nationally representative, experimental evaluation of Job Corps carried out by Mathematica Policy Research.[4] The study compared the educational attainment, employment and earnings, and nonlabor market outcomes, such as crime and receiving welfare benefits, of youth assigned to Job Corps to control youth outcomes. Job Corps participants completed significantly more hours of education and training and were more likely to attain a GED or vocational certificate than were control youth. Job Corps youth also experienced a significant earnings boost within four years of being assigned to the program, reflecting higher wages and employment rates.

These findings indicate valuable educational and employment benefits of Job Corps, which held across subpopulations of youth.[5] However, a nine-year follow-up report reveals that the employment and earnings gains lasted beyond the fourth year only for the oldest participants.

Lessons from program models and evaluations

Citizen Schools, After School Matters, career academies, and Job Corps are four unique approaches to career programming that illustrate a range of possibilities for support for youth. In this final section, I highlight three key lessons derived from these models that have implications for career development initiatives more generally.

First, career programming can and should be designed for youth across a broad age range. Career development is an ongoing process that begins in childhood and lasts through adolescence and well into adulthood. These models demonstrate how programs might engage youth and address their needs at various stages along the pathway from school to careers.

Programs for younger participants, like Citizen Schools, can introduce youth to a broad range of skills and careers, encouraging them to experiment and explore and start their planning early enough to make strategic choices regarding major milestones, including, in some districts, their choice of high school. As youth transition into high school, opportunities for exploration and skill building can be continued through programs like ASM and intensified through formal curricula and work-based learning opportunities in the career academies. Programs at this stage serve youth well by making explicit the relationship between developing career ambitions and the respective educational and training requirements. Assistance with the search and application processes for college and jobs is also critical for older youth, although this was not a noted component of either ASM or the career academies included in the evaluations.

Later interventions are also valuable. Programs such as Job Corps can reengage at-risk youth in academic and occupational training and help them get back on the career path. Given its emphasis on older youth, Job Corps appropriately stresses industry-specific hard skills in addition to generalizable soft skills, and it also focuses on placement in an appropriate job or postsecondary education program.

The second important lesson is that career programming does not have to come at the expense of academic training or preparation for college. Indeed, Citizen Schools, career academies, and Job Corps demonstrate the feasibility of providing both academic and occupational instruction. Career academies are perhaps the strongest example. The model dictates that students' vocational course work be integrated with a rigorous academic curriculum, usually college preparatory. As the work of Kemple and colleagues demonstrates, the academies yielded significant long-term employment gains without compromising participation in postsecondary education.[6] Academy youth enrolled in and completed postsecondary education programs at rates similar to nonacademy youth in the study and at rates higher than youth nationwide with similar demographic characteristics. These findings have special value within the current policy climate, where the dominant "college-for-all" mentality overshadows efforts to promote key nonacademic skills and competencies.

Finally, although each program had positive effects on participants, findings from the evaluation literature are a reminder of the importance of program quality in producing specific results. Weak or null outcomes could often be explained by evaluators' observations of weaknesses in the design or implementation of the programs. For example, the failure of ASM to contribute to marketable job skills, one of the program's main priorities, can be linked to instructors' lack of explicit attention to such skills in their interactions with youth.[7] As a second example, Schochet and colleagues attributed the short-lived labor market impacts of Job Corps in part to inadequate job placement services after youth completed their training.[8] As these and similar programs expand and develop, program providers must devote continued efforts to identifying and supporting the components related most directly to desired outcomes. In this way, more youth will have access to high-quality, effective programs to facilitate their career readiness.

Notes

1. Arcaira, E., Vile, J. D., & Reisner, E. R. (2010). *Citizen Schools: Achieving high school graduation: Citizen Schools' youth outcomes in Boston*. Washington, DC: Policy Studies Associates.

2. Hirsch, B. J., Hedges, L. V., Stawicki, J., & Mekinda, M. A. (2011). *After-school programs for high school students: A random assignment evaluation of After School Matters* (Tech. Rep.). Evanston, IL: Northwestern University.

3. Kemple, J. J., & Snipes, J. C. (2000). *Career academies: Impacts on students' engagement and performance in high school*. New York, NY: Manpower Demonstration Research Corporation; Kemple, J. J., & Willner, C. J. (2008). *Career academies: Long-term impacts on labor market outcomes, educational attainment, and transitions to adulthood*. New York, NY: Manpower Demonstration Research Corporation.

4. Schochet, P. Z., Burghardt, J., & McConnell, S. (2008). Does Job Corps work? Impact findings from the National Job Corps Study. *American Economic Review*, 98(5), 1864–1886.

5. An important exception is Hispanic youth. See Flores-Lagunes, A., Gonzalez, A., & Neumann, T. (2010). Learning but not earning? The impact of Job Corps training on Hispanic youth. *Economic Inquiry*, 48, 651–667.

6. Kemple & Snipes. (2000); Kemple & Willner. (2008).

7. See Alexander & Hirsch, this issue; Hirsch et al. (2011).

8. Schochet et al. (2008).

MEGAN A. MEKINDA *is a doctoral candidate in the program in human development and social policy at Northwestern University.*

This article presents findings from an evaluation of After School Matters, arguably the flagship after-school program for urban high school students.

5

Marketable job skills for high school students: What we learned from an evaluation of After School Matters

Kendra P. Alexander, Barton J. Hirsch

URBAN YOUTH HAVE difficulty gaining entry into the workforce. The problem is particularly critical among black youth ages sixteen to twenty-four who face an unemployment rate of 29 percent, compared to 15 percent for white youth.[1] Like all young people, these youth need opportunities to learn technical (hard) skills for specific occupations, become socialized into workplace norms and expectations, and develop and hone their soft skills—a core set of interpersonal traits and abilities that include effective oral and written communication, teamwork, problem solving, and project management.[2] Since jobs and internships for urban youth are scarce, interventions are needed that simulate a paid work experience and environment. These programs could operate in the after-school hours, a time noted for enrichment activities and positive youth development (PYD).[3]

Funding for the evaluation of After School Matters was provided by the William T. Grant Foundation, Wallace Foundation, and Searle Fund.

After School Matters: A possible solution

Chicago's After School Matters (ASM) is a large-scale effort designed in part to bridge the gap in employment experiences for urban high school students. Widely considered the flagship after-school program in the United States for this age group, ASM has served more than seven thousand students, mostly black and Latino youth from low-income households, every semester in recent years. It focuses on PYD and helps participants develop marketable job skills using an apprenticeship model. Each paid apprenticeship operates for ninety hours in a semester and is led by two co-instructors that have subject matter expertise but are not necessarily youth service professionals. Apprentices are expected to produce a final deliverable at the end of the apprenticeship, usually in the form of a tangible product, a presentation, or a performance. Many apprenticeships, such as in culinary arts and Web design, have subject matter that relate to common career areas. Other apprenticeships, like storytelling and African drumming, do not have an obvious link to a typical work setting. Despite this variation, all apprenticeships share the goal of providing participants with marketable job skills.

ASM evaluation

We recently conducted a rigorous mixed-method evaluation of ASM. Thirteen year-long apprenticeships, deemed by program leadership to be among the best, were studied. Outcomes were measured in four areas: PYD, marketable job skills, academic outcomes, and problem behavior.[4] The research team used an experimental design and randomly assigned interested youth to a treatment condition (participation in ASM) or a control group (no participation in ASM). This randomization helped to ensure that any impacts found were not a result of preexisting differences between students who participated in ASM and those who did not. We found that over 90 percent of youth in the control group were not simply idle in the after-school hours but were involved in activities including paid work, as well as school and community-based extracurricular activities. Here we focus on the aspects of the evaluation that assessed the development of marketable job skills.

Assessing marketable job skills: Mock job interview

Although interviews are an imperfect tool for assessing job applicants, the interview procedure remains the most widely used and accepted employer tool for hiring decisions.[5] In order to assess whether ASM met its goal of helping participants develop marketable job skills, we developed a mock interview assessment with help from senior-level human resource (HR) professionals. All youth in the evaluation (treatment and controls) participated in the mock interview, which was administered by volunteer HR personnel.

The mock interview protocol contained two parts. The first part included common interview questions designed to gain information about the interviewees' background, aspirations, and experiences and how they would react to hypothetical situations. The second part consisted of items that the interviewer rated after the interview, assessing applicants on a series of supplemental personal characteristics. This part included ratings by the interviewer as to whether they would hire a student if a job were available. Each item on the instrument was scored on a five-point scale using specific criteria to anchor responses rated at the ends and midpoint.

For purposes of the interview, students chose to apply for one of three positions representing typical entry-level jobs that a high school student might be qualified for and have an interest in obtaining: an attendant at a sports and entertainment venue, a cashier at a prominent public park, and a sales position at a fictitious retail establishment. Human resource interviewers who conducted the interviews received training and were required to achieve 80 percent agreement with consensus ratings prior to implementation.

Evaluation findings related to marketable job skills

Using hierarchical linear modeling, we found no statistically significant difference between the mock hire rates of students in ASM versus the control group. In addition, the ASM participants did not fare significantly better on composite measures of answers to interview questions or have higher scores on the supplemental skills rankings.[6]

Although no differences were found in the overall hire rates between the ASM and control groups, there was wide variation in treatment versus control group effect sizes across apprenticeships. In the most favorable comparison, one apprenticeship had students who were 47 percent more likely to be hired than students in their control group. However, there were also apprenticeships where the apprentices did much worse than controls.

We decided to study apprenticeships with two of the best and two of the worst effect sizes on the interview hire ranking. We sought to identify common elements among the apprenticeships with the best comparative effect size that distinguished them from shared characteristics of the programs with the worst effect size. We hoped that this comparison between extreme groups would provide a window into apprenticeship features linked to better mock hiring outcomes.

We analyzed over sixty sets of field notes using a grounded theory approach, each set representing one apprenticeship session. Some striking contrasts emerged in our analysis of the field notes. First, there was wide variation in the communications among peers (apprentice-to-apprentice and instructor-to-instructor) as well as hierarchically (apprentice-to-instructor). In addition, the professional orientation of the apprenticeships varied in areas including attendance and prevalence of tardiness, the orderliness and productivity of the work environment, and the level of initiative and self-direction demonstrated by the apprentices.

Communications

The programs that had the largest positive difference in hire rating compared to their control group (which we refer to as "best-hire" apprenticeships) were characterized by regular examples of peer collaboration and teamwork, exchange of opinions, and opportunities for apprentices to lead their peers. Instructors in these apprenticeships were also more likely to use positive instructional methods, such as correcting, teaching and coaching, and encouragement in order to achieve program goals. Apprenticeships with the most unfavorable comparative hire ratings, or "worst-hire" apprenticeships, were characterized by frequent use of negative communication methods on the part of instructors, including berating and unconstructive criticism, as well as widespread ignoring of problem behaviors. Interactions at all levels were more haphazard in these apprenticeships, including regular instances of off-task recreational behavior more characteristic of a leisure program than a work setting, and instructors in these apprenticeships were more lax in their enforcement of mainstream workplace communication norms. Instructors also were less likely to model professional behavior.

Based on these experiences, apprentices received different messages about what is acceptable and expected in a work environment. Instructors in the best-hire programs took advantage of opportunities to explain to students how certain behaviors could benefit them and related the consequences and repercussions to an employment context. Apprentices in those programs were more likely to practice soft skills that are useful in actual work settings. Apprentices in the worst-hire programs experienced situations that mirrored peer norms that are not acceptable in the workplace. These apprentices lacked explicit direction or examples to establish a new way of interacting. The differences could have an impact on the way the students presented themselves, as well as the types of examples that they could draw on in responding to interview questions.

Professional orientation

The best-hire programs had a strong professional orientation, where an orderly environment was maintained as apprentices worked toward a final deliverable. In addition, attendance and attrition were less problematic in these apprenticeships. Both of the best-hire apprenticeships also cultivated environments where initiative, independent action, and creative thinking among the students were ongoing core expectations. This was not the case in either of the worst-hire programs. Moreover, ASM youth in both of the best-hire apprenticeships engaged in sustained goal-oriented activity over a period of days, weeks, and even months. This was true of only one of the worst-hire programs.

These differences in professional work orientation should have an impact on student performance in job interviews. For instance, in the interview, students were asked questions about prior goal achievement and meeting project deadlines. Students in apprenticeships with a strong professional orientation could potentially discuss the regular performance benchmarks they needed to meet in order to complete the final deliverable, explaining in detail the steps needed to complete the project from beginning to end. In contrast, students in programs with weaker work cultures had fewer, if any, convincing examples from which to draw.

Workforce perspectives: The voice of HR professionals

After the mock interview experience, youth received one-on-one feedback regarding their performance. In these discussions, the HR professionals were often able to elicit information from the interviewee that could have helped the student make a stronger impression during the interview. Although this additional information could not be used to affect any ratings, the discussions clearly made an impression on the interviewers. In debriefing sessions, the interviewers told us of several instances where students discussed working on class presentations, leadership roles on sports teams, and community volunteering in the postinterview discussion but had not brought those examples up during the actual interview. The HR professionals considered these experiences and skills to be highly relevant to the workplace: they "counted" as work experience even though they had not been acquired in paid jobs. The students often had no idea that this was true.

These HR insights lead us to propose another interpretation of the ASM evaluation findings: many youth in ASM and in the control group may have shared a common lack of awareness of their work skills and thus, not surprisingly, an inability to communicate those skills successfully in the mock job interview. This is consistent with other qualitative findings from the evaluation, which revealed that most apprenticeship instructors did a poor job of explicitly communicating to students how the skills that they were learning improved their marketability.[7] High school students need to be able to answer the questions: What constitutes marketable job skills? How do my experiences and skills map to what employers want? How do I convincingly articulate this connection in an interview?

Conclusion and future directions

In response to ASM evaluation findings and a request from Chicago Public Schools, Bart Hirsch and his research team have piloted an interviewing skills curriculum in career and technical education classrooms. In the curriculum, students learn to identify job-relevant experiences, role-play responses to interview questions, and practice specific techniques to communicate their experiences and skills. The techniques help students develop elaborated answers that paint a picture for the interviewer by using convincing examples to strengthen the answers. Preliminary results are promising, with mock hire rates doubling or tripling in most classrooms between pre- and postcurriculum implementation. Plans are being discussed with school officials for a major scale-up of this program. The curriculum could potentially be expanded to other school systems nationwide and could help youth in the school-to-work transition if the interview skills they learn contribute to increasing the number of students being hired into internships and jobs.

More generally, in terms of what we learned about ASM, a rigorous evaluation revealed that ASM did not increase marketable job skills compared to a randomly assigned control group. Fortunately, the qualitative data we obtained as part of our mixed-method research provided clues as to how apprenticeship experiences might be strengthened. The qualitative data suggest a link between communication norms on the job, professional orientation, and mock job interview performance. Youth who participated in apprenticeships with communication norms and work-based customs that more closely mirrored mainstream standards fared better in the mock interview than controls did. In addition, HR professionals called attention to the need to teach youth to recognize their marketable job skills, regardless of the setting in which they are acquired, and communicate those skills effectively. These evaluation findings have already led administrators in one of the nation's largest school systems to make plans for changing the way they prepare students for job interviews. The findings can also inform the design and evaluation of other work readiness programs for urban youth, in after-school as well as school settings, and provide guidance for instructor selection, training, and evaluation.

Notes

1. U.S. Department of Labor, Bureau of Labor Statistics. (2011, December). *Employment status of the civilian noninstitutional population by age, sex, and race.* Retrieved from http://www.bls.gov/cps/cpsaat03.htm

2. Murnane, R., & Levy, F. (1996). *Teaching the new basic skills: Principles for educating children to thrive in a changing economy.* New York, NY: Free Press; Secretary's Commission on Achieving Necessary Skills. (1991). *What work requires of schools.* Washington, DC: U.S. Department of Labor. Retrieved from http://wdr.doleta.gov/SCANS/whatwork/whatwork.pdf

3. Hirsch, B. J., Deutsch, N., & DuBois, D. (2011). *After-school centers and youth development: Case studies of success and failure.* New York, NY: Cambridge University Press.

4. Hirsch, B. J., Hedges, L., Stawicki, J., & Mekinda, M. (2011). *After-school programs for high school students: An evaluation of After School Matters* (Tech. Rep.). Evanston, IL: Northwestern University. We evaluated these thirteen apprenticeships from 2006 to 2009. Since that time, ASM has made a number of changes to improve program effectiveness. See After School Matters. (2012). *Northwestern University evaluation of After School Matters: How we have changed.*

5. Rosenbaum, J., & Jones, S. (2006). "Interactions between high schools and labor markets. In M. Hallinan (Ed.), *Handbook of sociology of education* (pp. 411–436). New York: Plenum.

6. Hirsch, Hedges, et al. (2011). The findings are from an intent-to-treat analysis: a comparison of youth applicants assigned to ASM with youth who were not assigned to ASM. In a second analysis comparing youth who attended ASM for more than 75 percent of work sessions to nonparticipants, a number of statistically significant differences were found that favored ASM participants; however, the hire rate remained insignificant.

7. Hirsch, Hedges, et al. (2011).

KENDRA P. ALEXANDER *is a doctoral student in human development and social policy at Northwestern University.*

BARTON J. HIRSCH *is a professor of human development and social policy at Northwestern University.*

Youth enterprises can teach work-related attitudes and skills that open career paths to entrepreneurship and management for low-income youth.

6

Development in youth enterprises

Stephen F. Hamilton, Mary Agnes Hamilton

IN THIS ARTICLE, we consider why and how participation in youth enterprises promotes youth development, especially career development. We have adopted the term *youth enterprise* because it encompasses a wide range of practices and is reasonably self-explanatory. We mean by the term any enterprise operated as a business with substantial participation and direction by youth who are roughly ages sixteen to twenty-four. The literature related to youth enterprise is predominantly descriptive: it is about programs more than theory; empirical findings are from program evaluations. Moreover, evaluations are usually of entrepreneurship education, which may, but often does not, include the experience of actually running a business. As a result, this contribution is more conceptual and speculative than empirical. We make a case for the developmental affordances of youth enterprises and provide evidence when we can.

Youth enterprise is a broader topic than youth entrepreneurship. A youth enterprise might have been started by youth or by adults, and over its lifetime, it might employ serial cohorts of youth. Those postfounding cohorts miss the start-up phase; instead they maintain an existing business, just as most adult managers do.

Forms of youth enterprise

The simplest form of a youth enterprise is initiated and operated by one, two, or more young people but is more formally organized than such activities as babysitting or lawn mowing. Young people with creativity and determination can earn money by designing, producing, and selling T-shirts; providing DJ services; operating day camps for neighborhood children; and growing and selling vegetables. We attend here to enterprises that include multiple participants and have an organizational structure and an array of operations typical of adult-run businesses. The boundaries are admittedly indistinct. Some mom-and-pop stores operate casually, without distinguishing gross receipts from the proprietors' earnings, for example. Hewlett-Packard, Apple Computer, Microsoft, and Facebook have become icons of technology-led free enterprise with their origins in garages or dorm rooms and in the dreams and drive of young people. But icons are rare; more mundane and short-term businesses are far more common.

School-based enterprises

School-based enterprises represent another form.[1] They are explicitly designed as opportunities for learning. Although a teacher and sometimes other adults are involved, students fill many key roles and take major responsibility for the business. The business may perform a service, such as meals for teachers in a career and technical education school, or building and selling a house. These kinds of activities are protected from the free market. No one is paid a salary from the proceeds, rent and utilities are free, financing is not a serious challenge, and if costs are not recovered, no one loses. These advantages, in fact, reveal one of the limiting factors to school-based enterprises: if such enterprises actually enter the local market and compete with existing businesses, local business owners are likely to object that their taxes are being used to undercut their prices.

Franchises

A rarer form of youth enterprise is illustrated by a Ben & Jerry's ice cream parlor that operated for a few years in Ithaca, New York. Established by a youth development organization, the Learning Web, with assistance from the company and its foundation, it was a way to provide work experience for youth, including experience in management. In addition to the teenage employees, an adult manager was hired and a board appointed that included members with expertise in both business and youth development. (The first author was a member of the board.) Although the store was sponsored by a nonprofit organization, it was a for-profit, tax-paying entity. In fact, the store finally closed after corporate managers concluded that the market was too small to be profitable.

Youth entrepreneurship

Youth entrepreneurship is the component of our topic that has received the most attention, and we will draw on the literature about it. However, small business proprietorship and self-employment are usefully distinguished from entrepreneurship. Henry Ford and Steve Jobs are exemplars of entrepreneurship: they built what became huge new businesses to harness new technologies. But it stretches the category to include the owner of a convenience store, who is certainly taking some risks but not by doing something new. By definition, a franchise, like the youth-run Ben & Jerry's store, provides a complete package of products and procedures, requiring an initial investment and continuing management but forbidding innovation. Calling a street vendor or a babysitter an entrepreneur drains meaning from the term.

Promoting career development figures in the rationale of many youth entrepreneurship programs but by no means exhausts the reasons for creating them. Llisterri, Kantis, Angelelli, and Tejerina found, not surprisingly, that need is the motivation for entrepreneurship among low-income youth and in developing countries, while opportunity fits the experience of middle-class youth, especially in prosperous countries.[2]

Youth entrepreneurship has been especially popular in countries with large low-income populations; it was a key component of the move to create an "enterprise society" in the United Kingdom during Margaret Thatcher's administration.[3] Youth Business International estimates that 20 percent of unemployed and underemployed youth worldwide (those eighteen to thirty years old) could be entrepreneurs, but only 5 percent are.[4] Setting aside the imprecision inherent in such estimates, neither end of the range makes starting a new business a viable income-generation strategy for the majority of low-income youth. It can make a contribution by providing an income to a few and a valuable learning experience to more, but it is not a substitute for larger-scale economic development and for political and judicial responses to inequality. Around the world, entrepreneurship education appears to be the most common approach to preparing young people for either immediate or future careers as owners or managers of businesses.

Community Cleaning Service

The Community Cleaning Service in Mathare, a low-income suburb of Nairobi, was created by a group of young men with support from two U.S. business schools and the SC Johnson Company.[5] The advisors from the United States initially proposed an exterminating company. The young men responded with their own idea and organized to sell their services to clean shared-household toilets. The most common housing arrangement in their community is a four- to six-story building with five or six apartments on a floor and one toilet and shower on each floor. Because no one wants to clean a communal toilet, they often become all but unusable. The participants offered their services at a price low enough that all families on a floor would agree to contribute. As a result, the company prospered, the young men had paid work, and the SC Johnson Company provided cleaning products in bulk below cost. The cleaning company subsequently received a contract from city government to clean public toilets. Many of these participants have moved on into other jobs or to start new companies.

REAL

REAL Enterprises started in North Carolina in 1985 to engage high school-age youth in building small businesses both as an educational experience and as a means of promoting local economic development. It develops materials and provides extensive teacher education. Several state or regional REAL organizations operate in forty-three states and several countries outside the United States (http://ncreal.org). Today the experiences most young people have are more constrained, and less real, than when they were trying to build sustainable businesses. Their shift toward entrepreneurship education responds to the growing emphasis throughout the U.S. K-12 education system on didactic instruction in academic subjects.

Junior Achievement

Founded in 1919 as a means of teaching free enterprise, Junior Achievement (JA) engaged high school students in creating and managing small businesses. Today it operates in all states and involves up to 4 million students every year in the United States. It also operates in 122 other countries involving 5.7 million students (http://www.ja.org). However, their small business activity survives mostly in its after-school program, overshadowed by much wider participation in classroom instruction about entrepreneurship and business, usually offered by volunteers from the local business community.

Compared to similar students, JA participants demonstrate a greater understanding of free enterprise, receive more academic honors, and envision obtaining more education.[6] High school students in JA were less likely to be tardy or to miss classes and more likely to be employed both during the school year and over the summer and to engage in community service. The most striking difference was that 86 percent of JA participants reported that they were very confident about finishing college compared to only 12 percent in the comparison group. College students who had previously participated in JA said that the experience had encouraged them to go to college and to work hard and that it had given them useful information about both employment and academics.

Network for Teaching Entrepreneurship

The Network for Teaching Entrepreneurship (NFTE; http://www.nfte.com) has worked with more than 350,000 young people in the United States and around the rest of the world since its founding in 1987. The goal is to teach knowledge, skills, and attitudes that will equip young people to start and maintain businesses. Low-income participants in Boston gained entrepreneurial attitudes and reported more activities in which they took leadership and initiative, including business and other activities, than similar students in a comparison group.[7] They also showed gains in internal locus of control (agency, or the belief that they have some control over their own lives), which were strongest in one of the six high schools studied that had an exceptional teacher and among immigrant youth.

The NFTE study's findings about its influence on attitudes and behaviors beyond business complement the JA evaluations' findings about impact on knowledge about and attitudes toward free enterprise. Considering that the latter also found a positive impact on educational aspirations and behavior in school, we can infer that these kinds of programs can have both specific business career-related impact and impact in other domains. An earlier study of high school graduates who had participated in NFTE found that a remarkable 83 percent think of themselves as entrepreneurs and 87 percent plan to run a business in the future.[8]

Principles for youth enterprise

The features of positive developmental settings identified by the National Research Council's Committee on Community-Level Programs for Youth suggest guidelines to adapt to youth enterprises.⁹ They should be safe both physically and psychologically and provide appropriate structure, supportive relationships and opportunities to belong, positive social norms, support for efficacy and mattering, and opportunities for skill building, as well as be integrated with other family, school, and community efforts.

Youth enterprises can be considered a form of work-based learning. Some principles from that field apply quite well. The term *work-based learning* gained prominence in connection with the School-to-Work Opportunities Act of 1994. Based on our review of theory and research and our experience in designing and directing a youth apprenticeship demonstration project, that was one of the precursors to School-to-Work.[10]

Teach technical competence

High-quality work-based learning opportunities teach technical competence: the knowledge and skills required to work productively in a specific setting. In a youth enterprise, technical competence includes what it takes to be a good worker but also to be a good manager. Technical competence applies to a specific set of activities and procedures but has a broad base. For example, someone responsible for accounting needs to be able to process the kinds of transactions conducted by a specific business using their particular accounting system, but that competence presupposes basic math skills and an understanding of the principles of accounting.

Learn and apply academic knowledge and skills

Participants in a youth enterprise can both apply and learn academic knowledge and skills. Youth who do not do well in school can acquire and demonstrate a mastery of academic competence. Adults can help not only by teaching and reinforcing academics but also by pointing out the connections between activities in the business and academic subjects. Adults can also call attention to the critical value of postsecondary education as a means of deepening the knowledge of these subjects and point out various paths young people can follow after high school.

Teach personal and social competence

A major purpose behind creating work-based learning opportunities for youth is to enable them to develop personal and social competencies. Eccles and Gootman refer to these as "personal and social assets that facilitate positive youth development": life skills, vocational skills, decision-making skills, coping skills, conflict resolution skills, planfulness, commitment to good use of time, connectedness, and attachment to prosocial and conventional institutions, to choose only the most immediately relevant.[11]

Promote diverse teaching roles and behaviors

Creating these learning opportunities requires putting supports such as coaching and mentoring in place. These teaching roles do not all come naturally. Coaching involves not only telling but showing, plus explaining how and why, as well as questioning and problem solving, all in the midst of action. Multiple adults and experienced young people may be brought in to share their specialized knowledge and skill. Youth enterprises can be excellent contexts for mentoring, which, by our definition, emphasizes personal and social competencies, though coaching on technical competencies may serve as a point of entry for mentoring, a foundation for a deeper relationship. Mentoring in the context of a challenging activity has great potential for promoting youth development, especially career development.

Running a business with peers and adults is an excellent way to increase young people's social capital, including both bonding (with peers and others from their existing social network) and bridging (with people, especially adults, from outside their circle). Some adults, including the adult supervisors but also others with whom the business brings participants into contact, may become mentors. A clear message from international experience with youth entrepreneurship is that youth enterprises require continuing support.[12] From regulations governing the creation and operation of new businesses, to accounting, human resources, and many other aspects of business, youth running their own enterprises confront an array of challenges, which may be simple at first but become more daunting as a business grows. If young people are to succeed at running businesses, they need access to mentoring and advice and to professional support services.

Reflect about experiences

Running a business can give young people experiences that enable them to reflect and critically examine the practices and premises of capitalism. Simon, Dippo, and Schenke made a case that teachers should draw on students' direct experiences as workers to help them think about how the economy and society operate and about their place in both.[13] Their argument is consistent with Dewey's treatment of the relation between firsthand experience in the social world and students' learning.[14] The experience of managing rather than simply working in a business is potentially most influential on youth who are marginalized.[15]

Make career paths transparent

Participation in a youth enterprise should make a variety of career paths visible. Linking activities to career areas is a start. Communication about parts of the business that the young person may not experience directly but also systematic rotation through a range of roles and responsibilities can increase knowledge about all aspects of the industry. Productivity goals must be balanced by the provision of opportunities for wide learning, but the young people should also learn something about how people develop careers in those areas.

Vondracek, Lerner, and Schulenberg advocate an ecological perspective on the multiple and reciprocal influences between people and their environments.[16] Their life span view recognizes that people change roles and jobs over time and that these are developmental transitions as important as a young person's career plans and experiences. A life's work in a single occupation is no longer a likely prospect for youth. Their view of career development opens the process to intervention. Youth enterprises is an intervention that can reveal new career prospects to young people whose ideas about the future might otherwise be constrained by poverty, discrimination, and the lack of visible opportunity.

Conclusion

Youth enterprise is a promising practice whose efficacy has not yet been tested. The most thorough evaluations have been of entrepreneurship education programs, which are related but by no means identical. Encouraging findings from those evaluations and descriptions of ambitious and apparently effective youth enterprises warrant further program development and research. We know enough to be able to predict that learning, career development, and postprogram behavior will be related to the extent to which students engage in actually running a business, which in turn will depend on how the business is structured. It is possible for young people to do the production work without participating in planning and decision making or doing so in a perfunctory manner. Another strong prediction is that programs will be most effective when they combine a variety of components or emphases, especially instruction about the principles and practices of free enterprise, experience in actually running a business, continuing support such as advice and mentoring, and access to financing.

Notes

1. Stern, D., Stone, J., III, Hopkins, C., McMillion, M., & Crain, R. (1994). *School-based enterprise: Productive learning in American high schools.* San Francisco, CA: Jossey-Bass.

2. Llisterri, J. J., Kantis, H., Angelelli, P., & Tejerina, L. (2006). *Is youth entrepreneurship a necessity or an opportunity? A first exploration of households and new enterprises surveys in Latin America* (Reference No. MSM 131). Washington, DC: Inter-American Development Bank.

3. MacDonald, R., & Coffield, F. (1991). *Risky business? Youth and the enterprise culture.* London, England: Falmer Press.

4. Chambers, R., & Lake, A. (2002). *InFocus programme on skills, knowledge and employability* (Skills Working Paper No. 3). Geneva, Switzerland: International Labour Office.

5. Hamilton, S. F., & Hamilton, M. A. (2009). The transition to adulthood: Challenges of poverty and structural lag. In R. M. Lerner & L. Steinberg (Eds.), *Handbook of adolescent psychology, Vol. 2: Contextual influences on adolescent development* (3rd ed., pp. 492–526). Hoboken, NJ: Wiley.

6. Education Group. (2004). *The impact on students of participation in JA worldwide: Selected cumulative and longitudinal findings.* Colorado Springs, CO: JA Worldwide Headquarters. Retrieved from http://www.ja.org/programs/programs_eval_overview.shtml

7. Nakkula, M., Lutyes, M., Pineda, C., Dray, A., Gaytan, F., & Huguley, J. (2004). *Initiating, leading, and feeling in control of one's fate: Findings from the 2002–2003 study of NFTE in six Boston public high schools.* Cambridge, MA: Harvard Graduate School of Education. Retrieved from http://www.nfte.com/why/research

8. Network for Teaching Entrepreneurship. (n.d.). Brandeis University Research. Retrieved from http://www.nfte.com/sites/default/files/brandeis_university_research_0.pdf

9. Eccles, J., & Gootman, J. (2002). *Community programs to promote youth development.* Washington, DC: National Academy Press.

10. Hamilton, M. A., & Hamilton, S. F. (1997). *Learning well at work: Choices for quality.* Ithaca, NY: Cornell University. For a different set of elements, see Goldberger, S., Kazis, R., & O'Flanagan, M. K. (1994). *Learning through work: Designing and implementing quality worksite learning for high school students.* New York, NY: Manpower Demonstration Research Corporation.

11. Eccles & Gootman. (2002). Pp. 74–75.

12. Schoof, U. (2006). *Stimulating youth entrepreneurship: Barriers and incentives to enterprise start-ups by young people.* Geneva, Switzerland: Small Enterprise Development Programme, International Labour Office. Retrieved from http://www.ilo.org/empent/Publications/WCMS_094025/lang—es/index.htm; Chambers, R., & Lake, A. (2002). *InFocus programme on skills, knowledge and employability* (Skills Working Paper No. 3). Geneva, Switzerland: International Labour Office.

13. Simon, R. I., Dippo, D., & Schenke, A. (1991). *Learning work: A critical pedagogy of work education.* Toronto, Canada: Ontario Institute for Studies in Education.

14. Dewey, J. (1938). *Experience and education.* New York, NY: Collier.

15. Hamilton, S. F., & Claus, J. F. (1981). Inequality and youth unemployment: Can work programs work? *Education and Urban Society, 14,* 103–126.

16. Vondracek, F. W., Lerner, R. M., & Schulenberg, J. E. (1986). *Career development: A lifespan developmental approach.* Mahwah, NJ: Erlbaum.

STEPHEN F. HAMILTON *is a professor of human development and associate director of the Bronfenbrenner Center for Translational Research at Cornell University.*

MARY AGNES HAMILTON *is a senior research associate in the Bronfenbrenner Center for Translational Research at Cornell University.*

American employers should be key partners in any successful community effort to prepare young people today for the world of work tomorrow.

7

Building business-community partnerships to support youth development

Donna Klein

AT FIRST GLANCE, "businesses thrive in communities where youth thrive" could be mistaken for an empty platitude or campaign cliché. But at Corporate Voices for Working Families, it is an article of faith, one grounded in the firsthand experience of our diverse employer partners across the nation.[1]

Indeed, businesses everywhere have a compelling and vested interest in the quality of the labor pool from which they hire their employees today and their leaders of tomorrow. But on that score, troubling challenges await. As summarized below and detailed elsewhere in this edition of *New Directions for Youth Development*, a confluence of social, economic, and demographic trends has left a generation of young Americans—and the future American labor force—facing an uncertain future.

Too many young people today are unprepared to succeed in a knowledge-driven global economy. More than 25 percent of our youth—and in many cities, fully half of minority youth—fail to finish high school within four years.[2] Among those who do graduate, many lack the skills needed to prosper in the working world. Research by Corporate Voices and others documents widespread employer dissatisfaction with the skills and knowledge of newer employees.[3] Similarly, while most young Americans aspire to higher education, too few manage to complete their studies and earn a marketable degree.

The consequences of this education gap are growing worse. Leading economists estimate that two-thirds of all American jobs in the next decade will require some postsecondary education. By 2018, they project our economy will need 22 million new workers with college degrees, but at current rates, they will fall short by at least 3 million.[4] Compounding these facts is the simple reality of demographics: the huge cohort of baby boomers is reaching retirement age, with millions fewer waiting in line to take their place.

In short, America's education and talent pipeline is in jeopardy. Where will our future workers come from? How can young people today acquire the skills and experience they need to thrive in the workplace and in an ever-more-complex economy? And what are the appropriate roles for educators, youth advocates, and business leaders in addressing the challenges?

The art of partnership: Collaborating for success

Corporate Voices believes that in order to expand opportunities for all young adults and prepare them for the world of work, education leaders, youth development experts, employers, and other community stakeholders must build broader and strategic partnerships. Working together, community leaders who care about youth and the businesses that may someday employ them can achieve much more than they can on their own. This is certainly the case with efforts aimed at career programming and exposing young people to work-related learning opportunities in their time outside school.

For youth development leaders, partnerships with business can offer tangible assets. Most important, employers can provide young people with part-time jobs, internships, and other hands-on learning experience, affording them invaluable experience in the working world. Of course, employer partners may also help with financial support at a time when many youth programs have seen their budgets decimated. But community organizations should think beyond the standard asks for financial aid or fundraising and consider the many ways a respected business can provide local initiatives for young people. Businesses can serve as:

- *Powerful champions and advocates*, especially with legislators, funders, and local voters, which can drive broader support for youth investment
- *Change agents*, as school board members, community college trustees, members of the public Workforce Investment Board, or members of your own board of directors, for instance
- *Mentors, tutors, and role models*, helping local students and young people understand what is expected of them in the workplace

Similarly, by virtue of their culture, reputation, and expertise, businesses offer other strengths to nonprofits advocating for youth investment—for example:

- *Knowledge* about the critical skills and competencies that young people need to be successful in the workplace
- *Planning and operational expertise*, which may be helpful in program design, implementation, and marketing
- *Access to resources*, such as their own employees as volunteers, meeting or classroom space, or equipment
- *Relationships and credibility* that can be leveraged in seeking financial support or promoting programs with other business leaders and policymakers
- *Organizational culture*, by which businesses, with their entrepreneurial approach and focus on action, can help community partners navigate a new strategy or venture[5]

The business case: Varied motivations and the bottom line

Business leaders often possess the influence, leverage, and platform to change the odds for youth in their communities and help more young people reach their potential. At the same time, they understand that the challenges posed by their talent pipeline are not going to improve without intervention and that they surely cannot solve these problems alone. Just as youth advocates should rely on employers for their strategic assets, employers can benefit greatly from the content expertise, experience, and relationships of community partners who support children and youth.

In fact, the words *youth development* as uttered by an eager youth advocate will be heard as *workforce development* by an employer anxious about the skills of his or her current and future employees. To the extent that community partners can offer employers innovative ways to build a pipeline of young, new talent and address their bottom-line business concerns, they are likely to find a receptive audience. Beyond their workforce concerns, employers may find other motivations to forge community partnerships in support of youth:

- *Visibility and reputation.* A company may want to support community improvement efforts because it seeks more visibility on nonbusiness issues or wants to build goodwill—and market share—for its service or product.
- *Corporate social responsibility.* Increasingly, support for youth-focused initiatives may help a company meet its broader strategic corporate responsibility and philanthropic goals.
- *Social investment.* Far-sighted companies may prioritize their community work to make sure it addresses the root cause of problems, such as youth poverty or educational failure in communities where its employees live and work.
- *Employee engagement.* Interestingly, research has shown that a company's support for community initiatives can boost the morale and motivation of its employees, which can

translate into better retention and lower turnover costs to the bottom line.[6]

Building relationships in four steps: Business engagement essentials

Corporate Voices for Working Families has spent a decade researching and documenting the workforce needs of employers. We have also represented the employer voice within Ready by 21, a national partnership and set of strategies to improve the odds that more youth will be ready for college, work, and life by focusing community supports on children and youth from birth through early adulthood.[7] Based on this experience, we have produced a suite of research-based tools that offer valuable guidance for community leaders, employers, and others who care about children, youth, and working families in their communities.

Youth development professionals seeking practical advice on how to work with employers may find *Supporting the Education Pipeline: A Business Engagement Toolkit for Community-Based Organizations* most useful.[8] Published by Corporate Voices in partnership with United Way Worldwide and the Workforce Strategy Center, this reference guide breaks the business engagement process into clear, definable steps.

Step 1: Identify

As a youth advocate, begin by taking stock of your organization's capacity. What can you bring to a partnership with area employers? And what do you need from them? The tool kit walks users through a careful checklist of tasks for identifying business leaders most likely to support a specific initiative, be it out-of-school programming or anything else.

Step 2: Educate

Be prepared to educate business leaders about the most pressing needs of youth in the community with hard evidence demonstrating what is at stake. Statistics showing that youngsters are starting school unprepared, become disengaged, and drop out or graduate without vital skills necessary for success in college or careers will all help make the case generally. These data are even more compelling if they are directly related to your individual community or to the business leader's core market or industry.

Step 3: Persuade

The key to winning business buy-in is to speak to the business's specific interests. To secure a commitment that goes beyond the symbolic, you must articulate the benefits of a company's involvement in ways that show potential for meeting important business needs. For example, how can the partnership you propose help an employer build a workforce talent pipeline? Recruit more diverse candidates? Strengthen its own reputation? In short, how will a particular business's involvement offer a return on its investment?

Step 4: Activate

Make a direct ask of the employer and close the deal by offering a relevant, actionable partnership. Have specific targets regarding what you are seeking, but remember to be flexible and work with the business leader to shape his or her involvement and ensure it is a win-win relationship.

Sustaining the effort: A reality check

As important and potentially rewarding as they may be, successful community-business partnerships can be hard to build, and sustaining them over time can be the biggest challenge. In a study conducted by Corporate Voices to understand community-business collaborations, corporate and nonprofit experts alike identified four basic elements of effective partnerships:[9]

- Identifying a common problem and a shared mission and goals
- Ensuring a clear understanding of roles and expectations

- Establishing mutual trust and respect for the credibility of partners
- Assigning leadership and dedicated staff on both sides to manage the partnership

A key lesson learned is that business leaders will hesitate to enter into a relationship with a partner that cannot demonstrate it has the capacity—notably, the time and staff resources—to make the partnership effective. Because collaboration is a business risk, companies must have confidence that their nonprofit partner can deliver on its part of the deal.

Sustaining partnerships with employers ultimately requires a long-term engagement strategy built around mutual needs and interests. Whatever their motivation for supporting the effort initially, business partners will stay around the table and contribute as long as their needs are being met. And when those needs revolve around a skilled and productive workforce, the beneficiaries of successful partnerships can be our youth, our communities, and our nation's economic future.

Notes

1. Corporate Voices for Working Families is the leading national business membership organization shaping conversations and collaborations on public and corporate policy issues involving working families. A nonprofit, nonpartisan organization, it advances innovative policy solutions that reflect a commonality of interests among the private sector, government, and other stakeholders. Its more than fifty partner companies employ more than 4 million individuals throughout all fifty states. They are best practice leaders who have pioneered and promoted effective family supports, work-life balance, and education and training policies for their workforces—policies that often benefit their lower-wage employees in particular. Publications, research studies, and tool kits on a host of workforce readiness, workplace flexibility, family economic stability, and work and family balance issues are available at www.corporatevoices.org

2. Aud, S., Hussar, W., Kena, G., Bianco, K., Frohlich, L., Kemp, J., ... Hannes, G., (2011, May). *The Condition of Education 2011*. Washington, DC: National Center for Education Statistics.

3. Conference Board, Inc., Corporate Voices for Working Families, Partnership for 21st Century Skills, and Society for Human Resource Management. (2006). *Are they really ready to work?* New York, NY: The Conference Board, Inc.

4. Carnevale, A., Smith, N., & Strohl, J. (2010, June). *Help wanted: Projections of jobs and education requirements through 2018*. Washington, DC: Center on Education and the Workforce.

5. Council on Competitiveness. (2008). *Engage: A practitioner's guide for effective engagement of business leaders in regional development*. Washington, DC: Author.

6. For instance, Deloitte. (2011). *2011 Deloitte Volunteer IMPACT Survey*. Retrieved from www.deloitte.com/us

7. Ready by 21 is the signature initiative of the Forum for Youth Investment. For details, see www.readyby21.org

8. Corporate Voices for Working Families, United Way Worldwide, & Workforce Strategy Center. (2010). *Supporting the education pipeline: A business engagement toolkit for community-based organizations*. Retrieved from www.corporatevoices.org/businessengagement/

9. Rosenblum, E. (2005). *The art of effective business and non-profit partnerships: Finding the intersection of business need and social good*. Washington, DC: Corporate Voices for Working Families.

DONNA KLEIN *is the founder and executive chair of Corporate Voices for Working Families.*

In-school and out-of-school time programming should be reconfigured to support vocationally oriented learning.

8

Supporting vocationally oriented learning in the high school years: Rationale, tasks, challenges

Robert Halpern

THE STRUCTURE OF learning during the high school years in the United States urgently needs rethinking. Too many young people in our society lack access to the kinds of vital, productive learning experiences that will enrich their lives now and provide a foundation for adulthood. High school learning as typically organized is too fragmented, isolated, and abstract to meet young people's developmental needs. It is too fixed on century-old curriculum and pedagogy and too oriented, in an unreflective way, toward preparing young people for four-year college. Conversely, high schools have not been responsive enough to what we have learned about how young people learn best; oriented enough to the heterogeneity among young people in strengths, interests, and needed pathways; or sensitive enough to the wide range of roles, fields, and disciplines that make up our occupational and civic culture.

American society needs to move away from a standardized vision of learning during the high school years, and especially away from the tendency to view academic and applied learning in either-or terms. We need to foster and legitimize a diverse fabric of learning opportunities and settings for a diverse population of youth to help young people find the domains in which and means through which they learn best. In more direct terms, we need to sort out the role of vocational learning in this agenda. This will not be easy. Stakeholders in education and educational reform view vocational learning with ambivalence, if not suspicion, due to its stigmatized (and, by some accounts, stigmatizing) history, to concern for equality of educational opportunity (that is, the right for all youth to aspire to a college education), and to its perceived narrowness, which contrasts with the changing nature of work. Vocational learning in all its forms continues to struggle for parity of esteem with academic learning.

On the positive side of the ambivalence about vocational learning, there is growing appreciation that young people need access to a variety of disciplines in order to discover and develop interests and strengths. There is widespread acknowledgment that many youth need more vital and engaging learning experiences than they currently receive. Many, if not most, stakeholders in young people's development believe that they need at least some exposure to the world of work, regardless of where they think they are heading in the postsecondary years.

But granting all of these beliefs, we still do not want the aims of learning experiences during the high school years to be too explicitly vocational. We may want young people to be able "to find and act on who they are, what their talents, gifts and passions may be, what they care about, and how they want to make a contribution to each other and the world."[1] But in the process, we do not want to limit their options and possible destinies prematurely. In that light, there remains a sense that vocationally oriented learning is too directive and specific in character—a sense that specificity itself is "the great enemy of a liberal education."[2] The perhaps inadvertent result is that we deny young people access to just what would be most helpful to them: immersion in the fullness and complexity of the adult world—its places and endeavors, occupations and disciplines, problems and dilemmas.

Developmental basis of attention to vocational learning

Among the many critical developmental tasks of the high school years, young people have to choose how and what they want to learn in high school and begin planning for what they will do after, whether more schooling, commitment to a vocation, or both. These tasks in turn require young people to attend to their vocational selves: to confirm and disconfirm interests; think about and understand vocation (and vocational knowledge) in deeper, more differentiated ways; learn about vocational possibilities and understand what it means to be prepared for specific kinds of work; and understand how to prepare for work and the length of time that requires. Young people have to learn about and in some way practice the wide range of skills and dispositions that will be helpful to them in their work and further learning. They have to explore for themselves, but with others, the role of work and vocational knowledge in forging a sense of personal competence, integrity, and identity.[3] They may begin to explore how personally important work will be for them, what they think they want to get out of it, and what kind of work will fit their sense of who they want to become. Rehm describes this as developing "a guiding vocational narrative."[4] Choices about vocation are partly choices about identity in a deeper sense. As Higgins, Nairn, and Sligo put it, "When thinking about career paths, young people are asking not simply 'what do I want to do?' but 'who do I want to be?'"[5]

Young people are both curious and (often) naive about various careers. They report being interested in particular career fields but doing little occupational research or exploration (in part because they do not know how to do so). A large majority lack even basic knowledge of how much and what kind of preparation they will need for an occupation of interest.[6] Career interests often seem global and not rooted in either personal experience or opportunities in the labor market. For instance, a survey of youth in California found that 22 percent are interested in a career in arts and entertainment; meanwhile, only 2 percent of the adult population work in these areas.[7]

Data on young people's readiness to commit to vocation are contradictory. For example, one national survey found that "three quarters of high school juniors and seniors said they had tentatively picked out a career."[8] Yet a recent analysis of career aspirations in four cohorts of the National Education Longitudinal Study data set found that in general, young people in the United States are increasingly "directionless in their planning for the future."[9] Some youth "are aware that they are uncertain about their plans and that they are not engaged in clarifying them; instead they live on a day-to-day basis and hope that 'clarity will happen.'"[10] In general, young people come to understand only gradually "that they have educational and career decisions to make," in spite of how consequential those decisions will be.[11]

Social context for work on vocationally oriented tasks

The cultural and institutional context for vocational development in the United States exacerbates young people's own struggles with vocationally related developmental tasks. Adults (and adult institutions in general) play a critical role in helping young people plan and prepare for next steps beyond high school. Young people get hints and clues about possible futures, both further learning choices and possible occupations, from a wide range of sources. Some are informal and incidental, part of young people's social world in some way: emulation of parents' or siblings' choices, knowledge gained of parents' occupations, a friend's uncle who is passionate about horticulture or automobile engines. Others have to be formal and systematic, provided through key institutions and sectors of society, including schools and future employers.

Both informal and formal supports for work on vocationally oriented tasks are hard to come by for many youth. In one recent survey of a nationally representative sample of young adults aged eighteen to twenty-four, the majority reported that their high school experience was not helpful in preparing them for further education or work, including gaining useful work experiences and helping them acquire practical knowledge and skills.[12] Mortimer, Vuolo, Staff, Wakefield, and Xie observe, "Without structural bridges between school and work, [most] youth must rely substantially on their own resources."[13] Youth from disenfranchised families and communities face particular difficulties acquiring the supports they need. They especially lack access to the informal networks that might link them to valuable work-based learning experiences, internships, and jobs.

Schools are a central developmental institution, and it makes sense that they should play a central role in helping young people with vocationally oriented developmental tasks and try to be at least somewhat responsive to the labor market and trends in work. Work will form an important part of many young people's identities, connecting them to the public world and giving them a place in it. As a practical matter, some two-thirds of young people (100 percent of nongraduates and 50 percent of graduates) will enter the labor force when they leave high school, and they urgently need support throughout their high school years to plan and prepare for this eventuality.

Yet as Grubb observes, high schools seem oddly removed from both vocational concerns and the vocational world itself.[14] Schools in the United States "obscure ... the relation between what [youth] are doing now and what they will be doing in the future."[15] High school educators should, but usually do not want to, know what happens to youth "educated in particular ways when they enter the labor market."[16] Career and technical education (CTE) is conceptualized and organized as an elective in the great majority of high schools. Links to institutions outside the school are often weak; indeed principals, focused on issues internal to school life, feel compelled to keep the outside world at bay.[17]

The vocational role of high school has long been contested. Americans' suspicion of vocational education has roots in both our ideals of equal educational opportunity and the ways in which vocational education has appeared to thwart those ideals. Historically viewed as a fallback option for young people lacking aptitude or motivation to do well in school, CTE in recent years has been viewed at best as an anachronism, preparing young people "for low-skill jobs that no longer exist" and at worst as a subtle means of tracking youth of color.[18] It has been described as illiberal and mechanical. Even the "principled heterogeneity" for which vocational education is sometimes praised is argued to lead inevitably to hierarchy in the status of different subjects and focuses.[19]

High school curricula and learning standards reify a narrow band of disciplines and knowledge, even as it is clear that young people are heterogeneous in strengths and interests, that knowledge itself is heterogeneous, and that our culture is made up of a wide range of roles, fields and disciplines. Lerman observes that the narrowness of school curriculum stands in sharp contrast to a "strikingly heterogeneous" world of work, "with hundreds of broad occupations and within each of these occupations different levels of work."[20] The narrow range of school subjects not only makes it difficult for young people to find the disciplines in which they are most at home but contributes to the future loss of talents that society urgently needs.[21]

The departmental organization of schools makes it difficult to organize learning around domains that do not fit traditional academic categories. Bodies of knowledge residing outside these traditional domains, including those rooted in the occupational world, are devalued. High schools generally do not recognize the artifacts of different occupations as potential curricular resources. For instance, some two-thirds of middle-skilled blue-collar workers have to be able to read and create visuals: maps, diagrams, floor plans, graphs, blueprints, and so on. These skills could easily be integrated into a range of courses and learning activities. Yet high school curricula rarely provide learning tasks that require "integration of cognitive abilities with perceptual and manual skills," a key attribute of much work today.[22]

Pedagogy is just as constraining as curriculum. School days are structured to prevent in-depth engagement with learning material. Learning remains locked in classrooms, even though, as Richmond and Kurth argue with respect to science, it is inherently difficult to learn to practice a discipline outside the community in which it is practiced as a vocation.[23] Decontextualized learning is not effective for the majority of high school students or consistent with findings from cognitive and learning sciences that learning is most effective when it takes place in contexts that allow immediate application, where young people feel some connection to real-world endeavor. Barab and colleagues argue from the literature that to be socially responsible and scientifically sound, "educational or curricular work ... must enlist rich contexts and what is too often treated as non-academic content."[24]

High schools provide little vocational information to the sizable number of youth who enter the labor force on leaving high school, in part because their staff are ill equipped to do so and in part because educators view this outcome as a negative one. There is no parallel in workplaces of the well-developed networks that link high schools to college admissions offices.[25] Young people are not helped to understand what a first job means and how it can be an "opening to a future career."[26] In his interviews with students at a racially and socially diverse California high school, Conchas found that low- and mid-achieving students who did have career interests had no idea how to act on them and no help from school staff in learning how to do so.[27] These students felt invisible within the school. Reflecting on the large numbers of students pushed without any thought toward college, Rosenbaum, Stephen, and Rosenbaum note that "with our good intentions, we actually mislead the youth who most need our guidance."[28] At minimum, the sizable group of young people who enter the labor market after high school need some occupation-specific preparation during the high school years to ensure a constructive early work experience.[29]

A critical role for career and technical education

Career and technical education provides an obvious foundation for high school to attend more directly and fully to vocational concerns. As a bonus, the defining attributes of career and technical education are consistent with what the learning sciences tell us about the attributes of good learning experiences and settings, especially for middle adolescents. For instance, CTE recognizes and works with the heterogeneity of young people themselves in their strengths and limitations, passions and dispositions. It helps young people find a home for learning and growth.

A three-decade-long project to reconceptualize CTE has strengthened the field in a variety of ways that support its potential as a base for learning. This multifaceted project has led to refined and updated curricula, explored the potential of curriculum integration, broadened the ways in which CTE introduces young people to vocations, brought in more teachers with industry experience, created a variety of connections to local community colleges, and forged links with employers for provision of apprenticeship-like experiences. The solidity of this project is such that CTE proponents have begun to argue that the range of new curricular and pedagogical approaches being adopted within CTE should be harnessed for broader high school reform efforts.[30]

Participating in a CTE concentration gives young people a clear purpose for engaging in learning. There is now abundant evidence that the front-end model of preparing young people for the demands of adulthood—abstract learning first, application much later—does not work well.[31] Learning, especially the kind that challenges and revises mental structures, requires an active role for the learner with interaction with a particular environment in an effort to make sense of experience. CTE provides a vehicle for this process—a vehicle, in other words, for young people to use and make meaning of what they are learning. Theory and practice are integrated. Curriculum derives from the nature of tasks in the disciplines and fields involved. Young people work on actual projects and problems in defined fields important to the broader culture. Learning and producing tasks reflect problems encountered in actual work in a discipline and often reflect real-world constraints.

The curricular structure of CTE offers both depth and heterogeneity. CTE values knowledge and skill in a variety of domains, including those historically rooted in the trades. Its learning demands reflect the idea that there are different kinds of rigor, different kinds of thinking hard, applying knowledge, and being creative in approaching tasks and problems. Vocational learning is full of cognitive content, but of a different kind than academic course work.[32] In contrast to academic knowledge, which tends to be disembodied, vocational knowing "involves much more situated judgments and tacit understanding."[33] It tends to require the learner to "adapt what has been learned to different situations."[34] Especially as found in the workplace, vocational knowledge is often contingent, action oriented, and heuristic.

Deliberate exposure to work roles and specific occupations during the high school years broadens and sharpens the awareness of youth of the wide range of occupations (and levels within them), their conception of what might be interesting, and their willingness to test out specific occupational domains. CTE can provide them with knowledge "outside their immediate experience," contributing to a broadened view of both themselves and the world.[35] Some types of CTE experience (for example, in-depth internships and preapprenticeships) provide a head start for youth into competitive technical fields.[36]

Participating in CTE seems to facilitate different kinds of identity work. As noted above, it provides some young people a kind of home base for learning and growth. Meer finds evidence that young people "most suited to the technical track tend to gravitate towards that choice" and get more out of it and of schooling than they would otherwise.[37] It helps young people see and feel that postsecondary choices have to fit who they are and, conversely, that they do not have to conform to expectations that do not feel right to them. It leads to more grounded and specific planning. Whatever future-oriented guidance and advice that young people get in the midst of applied learning experiences seems to stick better than that provided out of context.

Good vocationally oriented learning experiences: A role for nonschool settings and organizations

As a complement to and extension of career and technical education, nonschool learning settings for youth scattered throughout American society provide an important source of good vocationally oriented learning experiences. Nonschool learning settings serve as both an important place for good learning experiences for high school–age youth and as a living laboratory for the design of such experiences. They illustrate why we need to look widely, flexibly, and imaginatively in considering how to strengthen learning during the high school years.

Sponsored by a wide range of institutions in a wide range of domains, four things seem most important about such experiences: their specificity (or particularity); their depth; their heterogeneity as a whole; and the fact that they take place in the actual physical, cultural, intellectual, civic, or occupational world. Sponsors and providers are not, for the most part, primarily focused on youth development; that is a by-product. These are experiences in which a young person has opportunity to learn and work in a sustained and gradually deepening way in a specific discipline, field of work, or service under the tutelage of, and sometimes alongside, an adult skilled in that discipline. Through that process, he or she begins to master distinct knowledge, skills, practices, and habits and perhaps also begins to acquire the social identity of one who works in that discipline or field. Young people may be viewed as students, service-learners, interns, preapprentices, apprentices, or workers, and they may be paid or unpaid, but they are always engaged in learning and producing something of real use to some sector of society.

Disciplines or fields define categories of experience. They reflect the full richness and diversity of cultural endeavor. In my own research alone, I have studied youth learning through the visual, performing, and literary arts; handcrafts, media and design; the range of basic and applied sciences; community development; environmental stewardship; entrepreneurship; culinary arts; and sustainable agriculture. And there are many more domains, some explicitly vocational—for example, health sciences, early childhood care and education, gerontology, biotechnology, information technology, construction, automotive technology and repair, engineering, aerospace, library and museum science, and law and justice. As implied by the breadth of fields, good learning experiences are rooted in an enormous variety of settings: studios, workshops and laboratories, hospitals and clinics, government offices, libraries, museums, theaters, bakeries, restaurants, urban gardens and organic farms, prairies and forests, on waterways, in urban neighborhoods and the streets.

The discipline or field, combined with the tasks at hand and the setting itself, provide ingredients for learning. These include specialized language; the norms, practices, and tools of the discipline; and its customs, traditions, distinct products, and performances. Adult mentors' deep knowledge of the field at hand, sense of intentionality, and direction provide strong organizers for young people's experience. Adult mentors and, in some settings, more experienced learners embody that discipline and serve as exemplars, modeling the practice, general behavior, and affective commitment of one with that particular identity. An adult mentor at Chicago's Free Street Theater (personal communication, July 15, 2008) notes that "there's always a diversity of skill levels in the ensembles. ... We're always leaning toward the most experienced practitioners and everyone else is sort of slip streaming with them." He adds that newer participants "gain permission to take creative risks by seeing the more experienced practitioners."

The curriculum as such is embedded in practice and production. Teaching and learning tend to occur in the course of the work. Demonstration is sometimes used to illustrate techniques and standards within a discipline. A film-making instructor might stop by a cluster of young people who are editing a video, see that they are not aware of a particular capability of the editing software, bring it up on the screen, and demonstrate its use. Young people learn by immersion and through direct experience, through trial and error, practice and repetition. The adult mentor from Chicago's Free Street Theater cited above continued, "They figure it out by doing it. You absolutely have to have the experience of doing it to get it. And we provide space for that."

Process and product are both important in good learning experiences for young people, and the two are closely tied together. Assessment typically is episodic; interwoven with learning, practice, and experimentation; and emphasizes the processes leading to a solution and the lessons derived from it, as much as whether it is precisely right or wrong. Mistakes are understood to be part of the learning and producing process. The specific field or discipline provides teachers and learners a self-evident, if embedded, set of criteria for evaluation, and often a ready-made means to observe performance. In discussing the fields of photography and ceramics, Albertson and Davidson note, "There are clear consequences if the technical processes involved ... are not properly sequenced or well carried out. Cause and effect are clear and absolute; no concept is good enough to survive poor execution."[38]

Regardless of field or discipline, good vocationally oriented learning settings provide key ingredients for meeting vocational developmental needs. They offer new places, roles, and purposes for learning, including opportunity to contribute to and shape the culture at large. They introduce young people to the variety and texture of the adult world. Through these experiences, young people may get a clearer sense of "what really is at stake in becoming an adult."[39] Good learning experiences provide background knowledge for planning and decision making and expanded, more accurate, and grounded reference points for aspirations—a more finite and, at the same time, more generous and concrete sense of possible occupational choices. Collectively these experiences provide enough variety of disciplines and social and vocational roles for most young people to discover their talents and confirm or disconfirm nascent interests.

Conversations with mentors can help young people better understand the pathway to postsecondary study or work in a particular field or discipline. Mentors can help them align their ambitions and better think through the mix of formal and nonformal learning and work experiences they will need to prepare for specific occupations.[40] As young people come to understand the work that they need to do to join a discipline or accomplish a particular goal, they can compare that to what they have been doing and plan to do in their educational lives. Mentors serve as sources of new social connections and may know the college programs in their field.

Good learning experiences help a young person see that vocations (and vocational cultures) are different from each other. Adults might share their own professional experiences, giving young people a more specific sense of what it is like to work in a particular field. An architect who mentors youth through the Art at Work program of Marwen Arts notes that he involves his young apprentices in some of his own daily activities in part because he wants them to observe how he thinks and works on tasks (S. Yu, personal communication, June 8, 2007). An apprentice to a plant geneticist learns over the course of a summer that a good part of doing science "is in all the hundreds of gory details, from how you pipette properly to how you make up the chemistry of a control for a particular experiment" (S. Strauss, personal communication, May 24, 2007). This gives the young man a much deeper sense of the day-in, day-out work of science.

A young person might be able to observe the range of roles in a particular kind of work setting. A young science apprentice observes, "Since I've been working in the soil bio-physics lab, I've noticed that everyone is working on a different project."[41] An oceanographer who mentored a young woman in her lab for Oregon's Apprenticeship in Science and Engineering program notes, "I tried to stay aware of my lab as a context for her [learning], to make sure she was exposed to a variety of projects and parts of the work, to invite her to seminars ... to see that there is a large field out there" (V. Chase, personal communication, June 28, 2007).

In a generic vein, good learning experiences can deepen understanding of what work is and what it means—its rhythms, distinct pleasures, and difficulties. Young people might learn that there are different kinds of days at work: good and bad, faster and slower, rougher and smoother. Adult mentors recognize the young person as a learner and are more likely to explain the logic of the setting, why tasks are done the way they are, why people relate to others as they do, why certain tasks are or are not important. They are more likely to teach the small things critical to socialization into particular work settings, for instance, "the cultural significance of tools and tool maintenance ... the rudiments of asking questions, seeking assistance, projecting a professional image."[42] Young people sometimes have an opportunity to reflect on the nature of work itself with mentors, for example discussing the idea that different kinds of productive activity have different social consequences.[43]

Systemic tasks: Building a scaffolding of support for youth

A broader framework for vocationally oriented learning during the high school years will require concerted work on three tasks:

- We have to locate, wake up, make visible, nurture, financially support, and legitimize the thousands of nonschool learning settings that provide their own important base for good learning during the high school years.
- We have to connect school-focused and more broadly focused efforts. We have to create scaffolding for a coherent set of learning experiences across time and place.
- Most difficult of all, we have to foster a culture of shared responsibility for young people, and one that sanctions a broader view of learning during the high school years.

In qualitative terms, ensuring constructive learning during the high school years requires careful attention from adult institutions—to the immediate needs of each learning experience and the coherence of experiences across time and place. Young people gain important experience and begin to grow up within particular settings, while the larger developmental processes under way in their lives can be said to occur across settings. As one study puts it, "The process of learning and identity construction appears to be located in between academic institutions, work life experiences, individual life strategies and socio-political contexts."[44]

Across experiences, both across settings and over time, adult institutions are responsible for creating scaffolding for growth—making room for individually appropriate pathways and ensuring there is a complementary, graduated, but intentionally connected mixture of learning, exploring, producing, and assessment experiences. These tasks require collaboration, shared responsibility, mutual learning, and mutual recognition across a broad spectrum of sectors that rarely work together in American society: schools, community-based organizations, juvenile justice, cultural institutions, single-cause organizations, the business community, higher education, state workforce development agencies, and trade unions and their training arms, among others. For instance, making youth apprenticeship work often requires the joint attention and cooperation of two, three, or more stakeholders—school staff, employers, and often community college or vocational training center staff.

The historic chasms between institutions, for example, between grassroots organizations and big public systems, and between schools and the business world have to be addressed.[45] Deliberate efforts will be needed to build trust from institution to institution, sector to sector. Institutions have to get to know each other, gain a clearer sense of what others have to offer (for their own work and for young people), and come to understand others' priorities and preoccupations. Individual institutions will have to recognize others' perspectives and sacrifice specific interests for a common interest in young people's well-being and growth. Institutions have to acknowledge different roles while not defining their own role too narrowly.

Different institutional systems will have to work to reconcile different orientations toward and views of youth, different learning goals, and, in some situations, different time frames for young people's growth toward mastery and timetables for their own work with youth. For instance, those conducting a study of an apprenticeship initiative in Toronto observed that community-based organizations, training centers, schools, employers, and trade unions each valued somewhat different aspects of the experience for youth: social inclusion, preparation for a particular trade or craft, providing an alternative pathway to graduation, and addressing local labor market needs, among other goals.[46] Employers wanted young people to prove themselves and their commitment to the trade by doing whatever was asked. Schools wanted young people to be trained for understanding so they would know why they were being asked to work as they were. The training centers wanted young people to have some breadth of experience to acquire a broader understanding of the occupation or trade at hand.

New roles and structures to increase the coherence of learning experiences

In the service of forging a more coherent sense of responsibility for young people, stakeholding institutions will have to convene to forge new structures. City- and county-level coordinating bodies, something like a reinvigorated version of the Workforce Investment Act's Youth Councils, would have to be created to spur stakeholders to commit to what is admittedly a very broad task.

Young people will need something like a learning home. This would be the place, setting, or organization that a young person views as the base for the full range of his or her learning activities. Because young people's developmental histories, interests, learning histories, and learning styles are diverse, they find learning homes in different places. Adults in these settings would have overall responsibility for the logic of young people's learning experiences during the high school years. They would have some responsibility for sharing information about learning resources in the community at large and linking young people to those resources.

It would also be helpful to think of the learning landscape as containing many learning bases—the settings in which young people link up with expert adults to nurture specific talents. These already exist in implicit form in numerous fields but receive too little attention as a deliberate means for helping the diverse population of youth grow. Learning bases can look and be organized very differently, for example, as a studio or workshop, an ensemble, an apprenticeship or residency. Schrag, for instance, describes a development called math circles (which he notes originated in Bulgaria and the Soviet Union), organized so that young people with a serious interest in math can meet weekly with professional mathematicians.[47]

A critical set of structures needing to be created might best be described as youth learning partnerships. Partnerships create a sum greater than its parts, in effect creating a richer, more varied learning landscape for young people. They introduce institutions to each other. They allow the strengths of each sector—schools, community-based organizations, industry, training organizations —to be extended by the complementary strengths of others. For instance, MECHTECH USA is an intermediary that has forged partnerships among school systems, community colleges, unions, and a consortium of manufacturers in Connecticut, Massachusetts, and Rhode Island to place high school students in apprenticeships in the machining and tooling professions. It has coordinated with educational institutions to create a defined course sequence beginning in high school and continuing into community college (for example, physics, math, technical writing, computer numerical control, computer-aided design, computer aided manufacturing) and oversees young people's careful rotation in six- to eight-month cycles through the many small shops that make up this field. The apprenticeship is designed to lead to a journey worker certificate and an associate degree in mechanical engineering.

Partnerships are often able to leverage resources, having a multiplier effect. For instance, nonschool organizations can extend the reach of school-sponsored career and technical education programs. Partnerships allow structured dialogue: those from different sectors share information and get to know each other. Youth-serving organizations often know little about local labor markets, and employers often know little about youth and youth development. As noted earlier, employers "typically do not have the time or resources to seek out youth on their own," but they might be willing to carve out a place for youth if they could trust referrals and help shape a planning and preparatory experience.[48] For instance, the Careers Through Culinary Arts Program (CCAP), a nonschool learning provider based in New York City, places youth as apprentices in restaurants and other food service operations. It screens and selects the youth and prepares them with knowledge of food safety, knife skills, and other basics. Employers have come to trust CCAP's referrals and know that CCAP staff are available to help with any problems.

Partnerships have to evolve "organically and pragmatically."[49] Different institutions and types of organizations are relevant in every city or county: charter schools, career and technical education centers, issue-focused intermediaries, and arts organizations, for example. Locally rooted partnerships are sensitive to local economies, local institutional strengths and weaknesses, and the distinct needs of local youth. As Kincheloe observes, "The resources of the local community ... hold the key to success for a critical integrated program."[50]

Conclusion

An important contribution of the broader learning experiences described in this article is to help us rethink how we account for young people and, in particular, how we understand their social role and potential contribution. The Australian concept of cultural democracy implies in part that young people are entitled to broad access to culture-making resources as well as to culture critiquing and consumption. The worry is that the press of the larger culture in the United States will undermine any effort to nurture new kinds of learning. Many adults in a young person's life and in the broader community have to believe in young people's fuller participation in the adult world. Without a clear cultural sanction, nonschool learning in particular is less likely to be recognized, supported, and valued.

Good learning experiences offer a vehicle for participation in the larger world. They address what Larson describes as a central societal challenge with respect to young people: "how to get this system of intrinsic motivation turned on and sustained."[51] They provide young people a chance to both learn their skills in the community and share their skills with that community. They serve as a means for young people to transcend societally imposed constraints, those encountered due to one's social class, race, or community of origin. As preparation, good learning experiences help make a larger world that often seems distant and monolithic more differentiated and human.[52] They provide youth some first steps into the adult world and do so in a considered way. The education director of Chicago's Marwen Arts notes of the youth placed in arts, design, and cultural organizations through Art at Work, "We send them out into the world to act as public agents, while they have the security of knowing there is support back here" (Lundius, personal communication, July 25, 2007).

Notes

1. Darling-Hammond, L. (1996). The right to learn and the advancement of teaching: Research, policy and practice for democratic education. *Educational Researcher, 25*, 5–17. P. 5.

2. Lewis, T. (1998). Vocational education as general education. *Curriculum Inquiry, 28*, 283–309. P. 298.

3. Lewis. (1998).

4. Rehm, M. (1999). Vocation as meaning-making narrative: Implications for vocational education. *Journal of Vocational Education Research, 24*, 145–159.

5. Higgins, J., Nairn, K., & Sligo, J. (2010). Vocational imagination and labor market literacy: Young New Zealanders making education-employment linkages. *Journal of Vocational Education and Training, 62*, 13–25. P. 14.

6. Mortimer, J., Zimmer-Gembeck, M. J., Holmes, M., & Shanahan, M. J. (2002). The process of occupational decision making: Patterns during the transition to adulthood. *Journal of Vocational Behavior, 61*, 439–465.

7. Yeager, D., & Bundick, M. (2009). The role of purposeful work goals in promoting meaning in life and in school work during adolescence. *Journal of Adolescent Research, 24*, 423–452.

8. Silverberg, M., Warner, E., Fong, M., & Goodwin, D. (2004). *National Assessment of Vocational Education: Final report to Congress.* Washington, DC: U.S. Department of Education. P. 60.

9. Staff, J., Harris, A., Sabates, R., & Briddell, L. (2010). Uncertainty in early career aspirations: Role exploration or aimlessness. *Social Forces, 89*, 659–684. P. 676.

10. Mortimer et al. (2002). P. 461.

11. Ryken, A. E. (2001). *Content, pedagogy, results: A thrice told tale of integrating work-based and school-based learning* (Unpublished doctoral dissertation). University of California, Berkeley. P. 79.

12. Roper & Associates. (2011, Spring). *Youth on education: National survey.* Storrs, CT: Author.

13. Mortimer, J., Vuolo, M., Staff, J., Wakefield, S., & Xie, W. (2008). Tracing the timing of "career" acquisition in a contemporary youth cohort. *Work and Occupations, 35*, 44–84. P. 46.

14. Grubb, N. (Ed.). (1995). *Education through occupations in American high schools: Approaches to integrating academic and vocational education.* New York, NY: Teachers College Press.

15. Hamilton, S. (1990). *Apprenticeship for adulthood: Preparing youth for the future.* New York: Free Press. P. 88.

16. Fenwick, T. (2006). Work, learning, and education in the knowledge economy: A working-class perspective. *Curriculum Inquiry, 36*, 453–466. P. 455.

17. Muhlenberg, E. (2011). *Who benefits? A comparison of school-firm partnerships in Chicago and Berlin* (Unpublished doctoral dissertation). University of Illinois, Chicago.

18. Meer, J. (2007). Evidence on the returns to secondary vocational education. *Economics of Education Review, 26*, 559–573. P. 559.

19. Lewis, T. (1998). Vocational education as general education. *Curriculum Inquiry, 28*, 283–309.

20. Lerman R. (2008). *Are skills the problem? Reforming the education and training system in the United States.* Kalamazoo, MI: Upjohn Institute for Employment Research. P. 22.

21. Noddings, N. (2007). *When school reform goes wrong.* New York, NY: Teachers College Press.

22. Kleifgen, J., & Frenz-Belkin, P. (1997). *Problem-solving at a circuit board assembly machine: A micro-analysis.* Unpublished manuscript, Teachers College, Columbia University, New York, NY. P. 5.

23. Richmond, G., & Kurth, A. (1999). Moving from outside to inside: High school students' use of apprenticeships as vehicles for entering the

culture and practice of science. *Journal of Research in Science Teaching, 36*, 677–697.

24. Barab S., Dodge, T., Thomas, M., Jackson, C., & Tuzun, H. (2007). Our designs and the social agendas they carry. *Journal of the Learning Sciences, 16*, 263–305. P. 290.

25. Bailey, T. (1993). Can youth apprenticeship thrive in the United States? *Educational Researcher, 22*(3), 4–10.

26. Reardon, R., & Balliet, W. (2007). *The work-skills mismatch: A review of the literature.* Richmond, VA: Virginia Commonwealth University, Metropolitan Education Research Consortium. P. 2.

27. Conchas, G. (2006). *The color of success.* New York: Teachers College Press.

28. Rosenbaum, J., Stephen, J., & Rosenbaum, J. (2010, Fall). Beyond one-size-fits-all college dreams. *American Educator,* 2–8. P. 3.

29. Goldrick-Rab, S. (2006). Following their every move: An investigation of social class differences in college pathways. *Sociology of Education, 79*, 61–79.

30. Bottoms, G. (2008, November-December). Promote more powerful learning. *Techniques,* 16–21.

31. Beckett, D., & Hager, P. (2002). *Life, work and learning: Practice and postmodernity.* London, England: Routledge.

32. Rose, M. (2008). Blending hand work and brain work. In J. Oakes & M. Saunders, *Beyond tracking: Multiple pathways to college, career, and civic participation.* Cambridge, MA: Harvard Education Press.

33. Grubb, N. (2009). *Vocational education and training: Issues for a thematic review.* Washington, DC: OECD Learning for Jobs. P. 21.

34. Billett, S. (2003). Vocational curriculum and pedagogy. *European Educational Research Journal, 2*(1), 6–21. P. 14.

35. Gregson, G. (1995). The school-to-work movement and youth apprenticeship in the U.S.: Educational reform and democratic renewal? *Journal of Industrial Teacher Education, 32*(3), 7–29.

36. Cantor, J. A. (1997). Registered pre-apprenticeship: Successful practices linking school to work. *Journal of Industrial Teacher Education, 34*(3), 35–58.

37. Meer. (2007). P. 568.

38. Albertson, C., & Davidson, M. (2007). Drawing with light and clay: Teaching and learning in the art studio as pathways to engagement. *International Journal of Education and the Arts.* Retrieved from http://www.ijea.org/v8n9/

39. Botstein, L. (2008). Let teenagers try adulthood. *NSSE, 107*, 118–121. P. 120.

40. Ryken, A. E. (2006). "Goin' somewhere": How career technical education programs support and constrain urban youths' career decision-making. *Career and Technical Education Research, 31*(1), 49–71.

41. Richmond & Kurth. (1999). P. 684.

42. Nelson, B. (1997). Should social skills be in the vocational curriculum? Evidence from the automotive repair field. In A. Lesgold, M. Feuer, & A. Black (Eds.), *Transitions in work and learning: Implications for assessment.* Washington, DC: National Academy Press. P. 85.

106 CAREER PROGRAMMING

43. Arenas, A. (2008). Connecting hand, mind, and community: Vocational education for social and environmental renewal. *Teachers College Record, 110,* 377–404.

44. pjb Associates. (2004). *Students as journeymen between communities of higher education and work* (Briefing Paper No. 50). London, England: Author.

45. Erbstein, N., & Heckman, P. (2007). *Locating support for disconnected youth in the San Joaquin Valley.* Davis: School of Education, University of California, Davis.

46. Taylor, A. (2006). The challenges of partnership in school-to-work transition. *Journal of Vocational Education and Training, 58,* 319–336.

47. Schrag, F. (2010, March 16). Nurturing talent: How the U.S. succeeds. *Education Week.*

48. National Collaborative on Workforce and Disability. (2005). *Strategies for Youth Workforce Programs to become employer-friendly intermediaries* (NCWD Information Brief No. 12).

49. Campbell et al. (2006). P. 24.

50. Kincheloe, L. (1995). *Toil and trouble: Good work, smart workers and the integration of academic and vocational education.* New York, NY: Peter Lang. P. 292.

51. Larson, R. (2011). Positive development in a disorderly world. *Journal of Research on Adolescence, 21,* 317–334.

52. Daniel, N. (2007) *Sweat equity enterprises: The convergence of design education, youth development and situated learning.* Dissertation submitted to the Program in Teaching and Learning, New York University.

ROBERT HALPERN *is a professor and chair of the Research Council at the Erikson Institute in Chicago.*

Career programming is a useful framework for thinking about how to support youth development across schools and multiple out-of-school-time contexts.

9

Next steps for research and practice in career programming

Kathryn Hynes

THE ARTICLES IN this issue of *New Directions for Youth Development* highlight the breadth of the research base relevant to career programming from which policy and practice can draw. In this closing article, I integrate several of the themes from these articles to highlight next steps for research and practice related to career programming.

Career programming as a framework in which many opportunities fit together

In education and youth development, trends seem to come and go. New topics receive a lot of attention, and programs and schools implement new curriculums, but soon another new topic emerges that grabs all of the attention. Thinking about career programming as yet another topic area however, misses its potential. Career programming is better thought of as a framework that may help us bring schools, community-based organizations, extracurricular activities, and employers together to support youth development.

If we keep youth development at the center of the discussion, youth need to acquire a foundational set of social and academic skills. Many of the skills that employers seek today—the twenty-first century skills described by Perry and Wallace in the third article—are called transferable skills by career advisors because they readily transfer from one work environment to another, allowing workers to change jobs and even occupations. Examples of these transferable skills are work-readiness skills like professionalism and punctuality, effective written and verbal communication, teamwork and collaboration, and the ability to understand and apply information to solve problems. These skills are not just important in the workplace, they can help youth establish and sustain healthy relationships and strong families. On top of these transferable skills, workers need to develop expertise in specific substantive areas as they move up in careers.

In reality, youth may be able to learn these transferable skills through a variety of experiences: classroom lessons, extracurricular activities, after-school and summer jobs, organized youth programs, community service, sports, and even helping their families. As Alexander and Hirsch (see the fifth article) find, human resource professionals counted learning that occurred in many different environments in their assessments of youth employability. To achieve beneficial outcomes however, these various experiences need to be high quality learning opportunities. But despite the different structure, funding, and goals of these experiences, the definition of *quality* across these different experiences is often similar. Hamilton and Hamilton show how features of quality youth settings such as mentoring from adults and opportunities to learn new skills can be an integral part of youth enterprises. Greene and Staff in the second article explain that "good" jobs for youth have opportunities to develop soft and occupation specific skills, mentorship from adults, and provide access to next steps. As Halpern argues in the eighth article, perhaps the goal is to help youth access quality experiences that let them deeply explore new fields and gain exposure to the adult world, regardless of which organizations or institutions offer the experiences. Utilizing a conceptual

NEXT STEPS FOR RESEARCH AND PRACTICE   109

framework focused on helping youth gain the various skills and experiences necessary for careers highlights the importance of working across domains.

Framing learning experiences in terms of career exploration and development may also help keep youth engaged in learning. As Porfeli and Lee show in the opening article, research indicates that career indecision can hold youth back. In contrast, research on youth engagement indicates that more engaging programs tend to link youth to the real world and help them learn the skills they need for the next phase of their lives.[1] Indeed, Perry and Wallace (see the third article) describe an intervention that uses career exploration and programming as a drop-out prevention program. Even for those not at risk of dropping out, career programming provides a framework in which children and youth can explore possible future identities while learning that if they want to be bankers, they need to do well in math class. As Halpern argues in the eighth article, the goal is not to constrain their choices early. They may ultimately decide not to be bankers, but the underlying math skills can easily transfer into a wide range of careers.

Focusing on career development also highlights important ideas about providing links to next steps for youth. Often an organization offers a terrific summer or after-school opportunity that gets those in the program excited about technology or engineering, but when the program is over, there is no next step or path for those young people to follow that will increase their knowledge and skills further. Articles in this issue indicate that one reason for weaker than desired impacts found in large scale evaluations of career programs may be limitations in these programs' ability to link youth to the next step. Alexander and Hirsch in the fifth chapter indicate that Afterschool Matters sites needed to pay more attention to explaining to youth how their skills would be marketable so they could access the next step, while in the Job Corps evaluation described by Mekinda in the fourth article, the authors noted the need for better job placement services after the program ended. To use Halpern's language, these programs might be more effective if they were giving youth the tools to move "across settings and over time."

Practical challenges, opportunity to introduce efficiencies, and gaps in our knowledge

If we think about career programming as a framework through which youth select in-school and out-of-school experiences that help them develop goals, transferable skills, and substantive expertise, then we need to consider the kinds of institutional supports that might be required. One way to implement Halpern's ideas about learning homes, learning bases, and partnerships might be advisors who help young people identify their interests and connect to opportunities available in the community. I use this hypothetical example of advisors not because I agree or disagree with the approach, but because it provides a concrete way to focus on the strengths, limitations, and gaps in our knowledge about how to move career programming forward on a systems level. I focus specifically on youth development outcomes and system-level efficiencies given the need to prudently invest limited resources in cost-effective ways.

Adding advisors to our existing systems would be another layer of infrastructure, and we know that pragmatically, advisors (guidance counselors, for example) sometimes serve more students than they can handle, making this good in theory but challenging in practice. At the same time, focusing on an advising model raises opportunities to highlight gaps in services and promote efficiency. Are all youth doing some kind of career exploration or career interest assessment, either through schools, workforce investment boards, or after-school programs? Are the results of those exploration activities tied to helping youth identify classes, activities, or relevant summer jobs? Focusing on whether individual youth receive these services could help ensure that more youth receive them, and identifying an organization to administer these services could reduce redundancy across organizations. Early on, however, we would need evaluation research identifying whether career assessments, and which kinds of career assessments, are most effective at engaging youth, improving their motivation, and helping them make good decisions about how to spend their time.

For this to be effective developmentally, these advisors would have to work with youth over time, listening to what they thought about their previous experiences, helping them update their career goals, and helping them select new learning experiences. If this kind of case management helps ensure that youth enroll in the next step, it could substantially increase the returns to investments in out-of-school-time experiences by ensuring that the shorter experiences youth seem to enjoy (one semester, a few weeks during the summer) are linked together in a string of experiences that together increase the time they spend engaged in connected, productive experiences. Evaluating whether this kind of advising led to an increase in participation in an appropriate next step, and whether the cumulative string of experiences improved youth outcomes, would be essential for identifying whether this was a cost-effective strategy.

Can we identify next steps that are appropriate for different youth? Porfeli and Lee suggest that we may be able to use developmental theory and assessments to identify where on the career development spectrum youth currently are and then help them select appropriate experiences based on those assessments. In a recent study of youth programs in Pennsylvania, we saw that some practitioners had already developed their own systems to ensure that learning experiences were at the right developmental level.[2] One program required youth with no prior work experience to take a work readiness course before entering any job placement; then youth were given paid positions within their own organization. This allowed the program staff to monitor the young people closely and provide more feedback on their performance. Only youth who had successfully completed this internal work experience were placed in job sites within the community. In this community, where youth had few work readiness skills, the program director felt this multistep process was necessary to ensure youth had the skills to succeed in off-site jobs. More formalized skill matching is also done. For instance, sports teams and some extracurricular activities like school plays use tryouts to match youth with appropriate levels. But to effectively match youth with roles at appropriate next steps would require a greater focus on identifying the prerequisite skills necessary for success in particular experiences.

This kind of system also requires the advisors to have information about all of the opportunities available to youth. In small communities, this might not be difficult. But in cities, this could be a real coordination challenge and might require a layer of technology and infrastructure that could cost more to design and maintain than the benefits it could provide. Of course, designing the system might provide an exciting technology project for a youth program to get involved with (and might ensure that the system is simple). And providers of out-of-school opportunities are increasingly participating in networks that are focused on facilitating this kind of information sharing and coordination through establishing databases of out-of-school-time programs or mapping available programs. As Klein shows in her article there are many ways to involve businesses in youth programming, and a concrete project like mapping community assets may play to businesses' strengths. In addition, many people who work with youth may already be investing considerable time trying to help the young people get connected to appropriate opportunities. Gathering the information in one place may reduce these redundant costs.

Perhaps most important, identifying the opportunities available for youth could help communities identify gaps in services and organizations that are well positioned to fill those needs. For instance, workforce investment groups often have information about growth industries in their regions, but do we have extracurricular activities, summer jobs, and vocational training preparing youth for these opportunities? Do youth have this information readily available? Transportation is a well-known challenge for youth programs.³ Coordination across opportunities might help reduce transportation challenges if all of the youth who need to be across town—for their after-school job, their out-of-school program, or their job shadowing experience—could go together. It could also be used to identify staff who have knowledge and expertise that could be shared at other programs. Having one staff person provide content knowledge on a particular topic for multiple program sites may be one way to maximize efficiency. But the kinds of coordination described here may run into serious practical issues related to the diversity of funding streams used to support different kinds of experiences.

Pieces of more integrated systems are already being implemented in a variety of ways. For instance, in 2011, the city of Philadelphia coordinated its summer youth employment program with the school system so youth could have a subsidized summer work experience and complete any summer course work they needed. Cities like Providence, Rhode Island, provide centralized information about after-school activities, and help coordinate activity schedules so there is less schedule overlap.⁴ Pennsylvania's Regional Career Education Partnerships system helps connect schools, workforce development, community-based organization, and employers in an effort to improve opportunities for youth. We should work hard to ensure that information about their challenges and successes is being collected and disseminated widely so others can learn from their experiences.

Conclusion

Perry and Wallace argue in the third article that we need a fundamental restructuring of schooling to align more closely with careers. There are many others who agree that fundamental reform is needed.⁵ In the meantime, focusing on career development highlights the need to ensure that youth have ample quality opportunities to explore their interests and develop higher-level skills, and that they know about and can access these opportunities.

Our tight fiscal climate requires that we allocate funds to the most cost-effective improvements to the system.

Notes

1. Hynes, K., Miller, A., & Cohen, B. (2010). *The Pennsylvania older youth out-of-school time study: A practitioner's guide to promising practices for recruiting and retaining older youth*. Retrieved from http://www.psaydn.org/Documents/2010PractitionerGuideforOlderYouthRetention.pdf

2. Hynes, K., Constance, N., Greene, K., Lee, B., & Halabi, S. (2011). *Engaging youth in career programming during out-of-school time: Lessons for program design from a study of experienced out-of-school time programs*. Camp Hill, PA: Pennsylvania Statewide Afterschool/Youth Development Network. Retrieved from http://www.psaydn.org/Documents/PSAYDNCareerProgramming.pdf

3. Hynes et al. (2010).

4. Kauh, T. (2011). AfterZone: Outcomes for youth participating in Providence's citywide after-school system. Philadelphia, PA: Public/Private Ventures.

5. Rosenbaum, J. (2001). *Beyond college for all: Career paths for the forgotten half*. New York, NY: Russell Sage Foundation.

KATHRYN HYNES *is an assistant professor of human development and family studies, and demography, at Pennsylvania State University.*

Index

Advisors, youth, 110–111, 112
After School Matters (ASM): description of, 4, 8, 45, 48–49, 52, 53, 56; evaluation of, 9, 49, 55–62
Albertson, C., 96
Alexander, K. P., 4, 9, 49, 55, 63, 108, 109
Ambivalence about vocational learning, 86
Angelelli, P., 67
Apprenticeships, in Citizen Schools model, 47

Barab, S., 91
Business enterprises run by youth: conclusions on, 74; forms of, 9, 66–67; principles for, 70–74; promotion of, 67–70
Business-community partnerships for youth development: benefits of, 78–79; description of, 9–10; and education gap, 77–78; elements of effective, 82–83; and employers' motivations, 80–81; four steps for, 81–82

Career academies, 38, 45, 46, 49–50, 53
Career and technical education (CTE), 89, 90, 92–94
Career commitment: description of, 14–15; in vocational identity status model, 12, 16–17
Career exploration: description of, 13–14; and identity status model, 12, 16–17
Career interventions, developing, 17–20
Career programming: defined, 1–2; as framework for opportunities, 107–110; importance of, 2–3
Career programs, school-based: conclusions on, 43; and dropout rates, 34–35; historical background on, 35–37; importance of, 33; models of, 37–39; in Ohio, 39–43

Career reconsideration, 12, 15–16, 17
Careers Through Culinary Arts Program (CCAP), 102
Carl D. Perkins Career and Technical Education Act, 37, 39
Chase, V., 97
Chicago's After School Matters (ASM) program: description of, 4, 8, 45, 48–49, 52, 53, 56; evaluation of, 9, 49, 55–62
Chicago's Free Street Theater, 95, 96
Chicago's Marwen Arts, 97, 103
Citizen Schools, 8, 45, 46–48, 52, 53
"College-for-all" mentality, 53
Community Cleaning Service, 68–69
Conchas, G., 91
Corporate Voices for Working Families, 4, 77, 78, 81, 82, 83, 84

Davidson, M., 96
Dewey, J., 73
Dippo, D., 73
Dropouts, high school: epidemic of, 34; in Job Corps, 51; number of, 2, 77

Early college high schools, 38
Eccles, J., 72
Education and work, historical relationship between, 35–37
Education gap, 77–78
Employment trends, current, 28–29
Entrepreneurship, youth, 65, 67–68. *See also* Youth enterprise

Ford, H., 67
The Forgotten Half, 36, 37
Franchises, as form of youth enterprise, 67

Gootman, J., 72
Grad Nation campaign, 34
Greene, K. M., 4, 7, 23, 31, 108
Grubb, N., 89

115

Halpern, R., 4, 10, 85, 106, 108, 109, 110
Hamilton, M. A., 4, 9, 65, 75, 108
Hamilton, S. F., 4, 9, 65, 75, 108
Higgins, J., 87
High school dropouts: epidemic of, 34; in Job Corps, 51; number of, 2, 77
High school years, vocationally oriented learning during: ambivalence about, 86; career and technical education (CTE), 89, 90, 92–94; conclusions on, 102–103; developmental basis of attention to, 87–88; settings for, 94–98; supporting, 10; three tasks required for, 98–100; and typical high school learning, 85–86; youth learning partnerships for, 101–102
High Schools That Work (HSTW), 39, 40
Hirsch, B. J., 4, 5, 6, 9, 49, 55, 61, 63, 108, 109
Hynes, K., 5, 6, 10, 107, 114

Identity status development, 7, 16–17

Job Corps: description of, 8, 45–46, 51–52; lessons from, 53, 54, 109
Job skills: marketable, 9, 53–54, 55–62; soft, 24, 27, 48, 53, 59; twenty-first-century, 34–35, 108
Jobs, S., 67
Junior Achievement (JA), 69–70

Kantis, H., 67
Kemple, J. J., 50, 53
Kincheloe, L., 102
Klein, D., 4, 9, 77, 84, 112
Kurth, A., 91

Larson, R., 103
Lee, B., 3, 7, 11, 22, 109, 111
Lerman, R., 90
Lerner, R. M., 73
Llisterri, J. J., 67
Lundius, 103

Making My Future Work (MMFW), 41–42
MC²STEM High School, 40–41
MECHTECH USA, 101
Meer, J., 93

Mekinda, M. A., 4, 8, 45, 54, 109
Monitoring the Future Study, 7, 25, 26, 28
Mortimer, J., 89

Nairn, K., 87
A Nation at Risk, 36
Network for Teaching Entrepreneurship (NFTE), 70

Partnership for 21st Century Skills (P21), 34–35
Partnerships, youth learning, 101–102
Pathways to Prosperity Project, 38
Pennsylvania's Regional Career Education Partnerships system, 113
Perkins Career and Technical Education Act, 37, 39
Perkins Vocational Education Act of 1984, 37
Perry, J. C., 4, 8, 33, 44, 108, 109, 113
Personal and social competence, 72
Porfeli, E. J., 3, 7, 11, 22, 109, 111
Positive youth development (PYD), 49, 55, 56

Ready by 21, 81, 84
REAL Enterprises, 69
Rehm, M., 87
Richmond, G., 91
Rosenbaum, J., 91
Rosenbaum, J., 91

Schenke, A., 73
Schochet, P. Z., 54
School-based career programs: conclusions on, 43; and dropout rates, 34–35; historical background on, 35–37; importance of, 33; models of, 37–39; in Ohio, 39–43
School-based enterprises, 66
School-to-Work Opportunities Act (STWOA) of 1994, 37, 42, 71
Schrag, F., 101
Schulenberg, J. E., 73
Simon, R. I., 73
Skills: marketable, 9, 53–54, 55–62; soft, 24, 27, 48, 53, 59; twenty-first-century, 34–35, 108
Sligo, J., 87
Smith-Hughes Act of 1917, 35

Soft skills, development of, 24, 27, 48, 53, 59
Sports participation, and teenage employment, 26, 27
Staff, J., 4, 7, 23, 31, 89, 108
Stephen, J., 91
Strauss, S., 97
Supporting the Education Pipeline: A Business Engagement Toolkit for Community-Based Organizations, 81

Technical preparation programs, 38. *See also* Career and technical education (CTE); Vocationally oriented learning
Teenagers: early workplace experiences of, 25–28; and sports participation, 26, 27; unemployment rate of, 28–29; working hours of, 24–25
Tejerina, L., 67
Thatcher, M., 68
Transferable skills, 108, 110
TV viewing, and youth employment, 26
Twenty-first-century skills, 34–35, 108

Unemployment rate of teenagers, 28

Vocational Identity Status Assessment, 18
Vocational identity status model, 12, 16–17
Vocationally oriented learning: ambivalence about, 86; career and technical education (CTE), 89, 90, 92–94; conclusions on, 102–103; developmental basis of attention to, 87–88; settings for, 94–98; supporting, 10; three tasks required for, 98–100; and typical high school learning, 85–86; youth learning partnerships for, 100–102
Vocationally oriented tasks, social context for work on, 88–91
Vondracek, F. W., 73
Vuolo, M., 89

Wakefield, S., 89
Wallace, E. W., 4, 8, 33, 44, 108, 109, 113
Work and education, historical relationship between, 35–37
Workforce Investment Act's Youth Councils, 100
Working hours of teenagers, 24–25
Workplace: early experiences in, 25–28; entering the, 24–25

Xie, W., 89

Youth enterprise: conclusions on, 74; defined, 65; forms of, 9, 66–67; principles for, 70–74; promotion of, 67–70
Yu, S., 97

NEW DIRECTIONS FOR YOUTH DEVELOPMENT
ORDER FORM SUBSCRIPTION AND SINGLE ISSUES

DISCOUNTED BACK ISSUES:

Use this form to receive 20% off all back issues of *New Directions for Youth Development*.
All single issues priced at **$23.20** (normally $29.00).

TITLE	ISSUE NO.	ISBN
_____	_____	_____
_____	_____	_____

Call 888-378-2537 or see mailing instructions below. When calling, mention the promotional code JBNND to receive your discount. For a complete list of issues, please visit www.josseybass.com/go/ndyd

SUBSCRIPTIONS: (1 YEAR, 4 ISSUES)

☐ New Order   ☐ Renewal

U.S.	☐ Individual: $89	☐ Institutional: $281
CANADA/MEXICO	☐ Individual: $89	☐ Institutional: $321
ALL OTHERS	☐ Individual: $113	☐ Institutional: $355

Call 888-378-2537 or see mailing and pricing instructions below.
Online subscriptions are available at www.onlinelibrary.wiley.com

ORDER TOTALS:

Issue / Subscription Amount: $ _____
Shipping Amount: $ _____
(for single issues only – subscription prices include shipping)
Total Amount: $ _____

SHIPPING CHARGES:
First Item $6.00
Each Add'l Item $2.00

(No sales tax for U.S. subscriptions. Canadian residents, add GST for subscription orders. Individual rate subscriptions must be paid by personal check or credit card. Individual rate subscriptions may not be resold as library copies.)

BILLING & SHIPPING INFORMATION:

☐ **PAYMENT ENCLOSED:** *(U.S. check or money order only. All payments must be in U.S. dollars.)*
☐ **CREDIT CARD:** ☐ VISA ☐ MC ☐ AMEX

Card number _____ Exp. Date _____
Card Holder Name _____ Card Issue # _____
Signature _____ Day Phone _____

☐ **BILL ME:** *(U.S. institutional orders only. Purchase order required.)*
Purchase order # _____
Federal Tax ID 13559302 • GST 89102-8052

Name _____
Address _____
Phone _____ E-mail _____

Copy or detach page and send to: John Wiley & Sons, One Montgomery Street, Suite 1200, San Francisco, CA 94104-4594
Order Form can also be faxed to: 888-481-2665

PROMO JBNND

Notes for Contributors

After reading this issue, you might be interested in becoming a contributor to *New Directions for Youth Development: Theory, Practice, and Research*. In the tradition of the New Directions series, each volume of the journal addresses a single, timely topic, although special issues covering a variety of topics are occasionally commissioned. Submissions should address the implications of theory for practice and research directions, and how these arenas can better inform one another. Articles may focus on any aspect of youth development; all theoretical and methodological orientations are welcome.

If you would like to serve as an issue editor, you can email the editor-in-chief, Gil Noam, at Gil_Noam@harvard.edu. If he approves of your idea, the next step would be to submit an outline of no more than three pages that includes a brief description of your proposed topic and its significance, along with a brief synopsis of individual articles (including tentative authors and a working title for each chapter).

If you are interested in contributing an individual article, please contact the managing editor Erin Cooney at ecooney@mclean.harvard.edu first to see whether the topic will fit with any of the upcoming issues. The upcoming issues are listed on our Web site, www.pearweb.org/ndyd. If the article does fit topically, the managing editor will send you guidelines for submission.

For all prospective issue editors:

- Please make sure to keep accessibility in mind, by illustrating theoretical ideas with specific examples and explaining technical terms in nontechnical language. A busy practitioner who may

not have an extensive research background should be well served by our work.
- Please keep in mind that references should be limited to twentyfive to thirty per article. Authors should make use of case examples to illustrate their ideas, rather than citing exhaustive research references. For readers who want to delve more deeply into a particular topic, you and/or chapter authors may want to recommend two or three key articles, books, or Web sites that are influential in the field, to be featured on a resource page.
- All reference information should be listed as endnotes, rather than including author names in the body of the article or footnotes at the bottom of the page. The endnotes are in APA style.
- Please visit http://www.pearweb.org for more information.

Gil G. Noam
Editor-in-Chief